# The Secret to Perfect Living

## Kofi Dwira

GoToPublish LLC
1-888-337-1724
www.gotopublish.com
info@gotopublish.com

# CONTENTS


Preface ........................................ v
A Special Note to the Readers ........................... vii
Where is the Secret? ..................................1
What is the Secret? .................................. 5
The Way to Love ...................................13
The Way to Life....................................17
The Way to Peace...................................21
The Way to the Character of God ...................... 25
Humility: The Precious Pearl of God ...................31
The Way to Patience.................................37
The Vocation of the Perfect Life ......................41
The Way to Destroy the Devil and His Works .....47
Why Suffering ....................................51
God's Sign to Perfect Living ........................67
The Principle of the Perfect Life......................81
The Number Seven and Perfection.................... 93
God's Seal or Satan's Mark..........................117
Applying the Secret.................................147
My Testimony ....................................167

# PREFACE

Many times, when men are faced with a problem for which they have no answer, they resolve into thinking that the problem is insurmountable.

The Bible calls Christians into perfect and holy living; but because, as sinners, perfection has eluded us, we have resolved into thinking that perfection is unattainable to men. We even stigmatize the proponents of perfection and view them as extremists and perfectionists, while failing to realize, if Jesus lived in our time, we would stigmatize him as such. Let us not forget that Adam and Eve before they sinned lived perfectly. There was no stain of sin nor weakness in their characters but they lived wholly abiding by the word and power of God. The same is said about Lucifer. God speaks about Lucifer, the originator of sin, and says: "Thou wast perfect in thy ways from the day that thou wast created, till iniquity was found in thee." (Ezek. 28:15 KJV)

Jesus, who came to be our example to living a sinless life, was born into our world with the possibility to sin. The Scripture says: "He was numbered with the transgressors" (lsa. 53:12 KJV). We recall he was tempted by the devil, as we are tempted; but he never sinned. The Scriptures testifying to the perfect life of Jesus, says of him: "For we have not an high priest which cannot be touched with the feeling of our infirmities; but was in all points tempted like as we are, yet without sin" (Heb. 4:15 KJV).

It is Jesus who said, "Be ye therefore perfect, even as your Father which is in heaven is perfect." (Matt. 5:48 KJV) In other words, Jesus was saying, "Be sinless as your Father who is in heaven is sinless."

The secret to the perfect life of Jesus, living in a world polluted with sin and with an enemy who tempts at every step of the way, is that there is a way to living a perfect life. And this is the way by which Jesus lived and never sinned. The question we may ask, as Christians who seek to be like Jesus, is: How did he do it?

It was only as Jesus came to live in our world and to teach by precept and example that God's way to living a life without sin was unfolded before the whole universe. Even until then, the angels of heaven, though sinless, did not have full knowledge of the way of God, as to how one could live in a world of sin and not sin. The Scriptures say the angels desire to look into the things pertaining to our salvation.

It is possible for us to live the perfect life, which Jesus lived here on earth. If you want to know the way by which Jesus lived and never sinned and desire to be victorious over every sin and reflect perfectly the character of Christ, then this book is for you.

# A SPECIAL NOTE TO THE READERS

The Controversy between good and evil, between God and Satan, evolves around how to be like God.

The angel Lucifer, who had desired to be like God in heaven, had claimed to have a better way to be like God when he approached Eve in the Garden of Eden. Satan, speaking to Eve through the serpent about the Tree of the Knowledge of good and evil, had said to her: "You will not surely die. For God knows that in the day you eat of it your eyes will be opened, and you will be like God, knowing good and evil" (Genesis 3:4-5 NKJV).

Could Satan, who came in the guise of a serpent, be right? Could his way of being like God be right?

In this book you will find the sure way to be like God, and, thus, the secret to perfect living. This is the greatest discovery that could ever be made in the whole universe.

# WHERE IS THE SECRET?

The secret to living a perfect life is all to be found in the Christian sacrament of baptism. That ritual, which symbolizes the death to our old lives and the birth of our new life found in Jesus, is the key that unlocks the secret to living the perfect, Christian life. In other words, the real meaning of baptism is the way to living a life without sin.

What then is baptism? The word *baptism*, which originates from the Greek word *baptizo*, means to submerge or immerse. When something is hidden in the earth, it is said of that thing that it is buried in the earth. And when something is hidden in water, it is said to be submerged or immersed in water. Baptism, which takes place in water, will, therefore, mean to hide or bury in water. Somehow it is clearly defined by the apostle Paul, who wrote much about it. In his epistle to the Romans, Paul says: "Know ye not, that so many of us as were baptized into Jesus Christ were baptized into his death? Therefore we are buried with him by baptism into death..." (Rom. 6:3-4 KJV).

In Paul's definition of baptism is supplied the word death. What then is the purpose of baptism? Paul says, "We are buried with him (Christ) by baptism into death... Knowing this, that our old man is crucified with him, that the body of sin might be destroyed, that henceforth we should not serve sin. For he that is dead is freed from sin" (Rom. 6:4, 6, 7 KJV). The purpose of baptism, therefore, is to destroy or put to death our old man of sin.

We may ask the question: what constitutes death? The wise man, Solomon, says:

> For the living know that they shall die: but the dead know not any thing, neither have they any more a reward; for the memory of them is forgotten. Also their love, and their hatred, and their envy, is now perished; neither have they any more a portion for ever in any thing that is done under the sun (Eccles. 9:5-6 KJV).

In other words, at death, man loses his senses of sight, hearing, reasoning, taste, and feeling, and also his portion in the things of the earth. The means through which sin appeals to us is through our senses. Therefore, if we are to overcome sin, we have to put to death our senses.

It is through the principle of baptism that we are to overcome sin. Baptism therefore is not just a ritual but the symbol and visual aid of the principle that should be the guiding rule in the life of the child of God. This principle is dying to sin and arising daily to live unto righteousness. The apostle Paul expounds the principle of baptism and says: "What shall we say then? Shall we continue in sin, that grace may abound? God forbid. How shall we that are dead to sin live any longer therein? Know ye not that so many of us as were baptized into Jesus Christ were baptized into his death? Therefore we are buried with him by baptism into death: that like as Christ was raised up from the dead by the glory of the Father, even so we also should walk in newness of life. For if we have been planted together in the likeness of his death, we shall be also in the likeness of his resurrection: knowing this, that our old man is crucified with him, that the body of sin might be destroyed, that henceforth we should not serve sin. For he that is dead is freed from sin. Now if we be dead with Christ, we believe that we shall also live with him: knowing that Christ being raised from the dead dieth no more; death hath no more dominion over him. For in that he died, he died unto sin once: but in that he liveth, he liveth unto God. Likewise reckon ye also yourselves to be dead indeed unto sin, but alive unto God through Jesus Christ our Lord. Let not sin therefore reign in your mortal body, that ye should obey it in the lusts thereof. Neither yield ye your members as instruments of unrighteousness unto sin: but yield yourselves unto God, as those that are alive from the dead, and your members as instruments of righteousness unto God. For sin shall not have dominion over you; for ye are not under the law, but under grace." (Rom, 6:1-14, KJV)

The principle of baptism, which is death to sin, but alive unto righteousness, is the principle by which Jesus lived and never sinned. This is the principle by which God lives. It was therefore in demonstrating the principle by which God lives, and setting it as the example to be exemplified in the life of every believer that Jesus was baptized. And it is by this principle that the child of God is to live to form a character patterned after the character of God.

# WHAT IS THE SECRET?

We know Satan is the enemy of man. He is the one who seeks to destroy every man with his weapon, sin. But surprisingly Satan and sin are not the greatest enemies of man. The greatest enemy of man is man himself, or what we call, self. We are our own terrible foes. Why? Because Satan can only suggest to man what to do. But he cannot make man do according to his bidding, against the will of man. Of course the unregenerate heart cannot but yield to the prompting of Satan, because it does not have the power, which power is the Holy Spirit, to withstand temptation. For the fact we are our own worst enemies, there is the need for us to destroy our greatest enemy, self.

Within ourselves we are unable to perform the righteous works of God. Having become slaves to Satan and sin, we are unable to free ourselves. So the apostle, Paul, speaking about the condition of sinful man, says:

For that which I do I allow not: for what I would, that do I not; but what I hate, that do I. If then I do that which I would not, I consent unto the law that it is good. Now then it is no more I that do it, but sin that dwelleth in me. For I know that in me (that is, in my flesh) dwelleth no good thing: for to will is present with me: but how to perform that which is good I find not. For the good that I would I do not: but the evil which I would not that I do. Now if I do that I would not, it is no more I that do it, but sin that dwelleth in me. I find then a law, that, when I would do good, evil is present with me. For I delight in the law of God after the inward man: But I see another law in my members, warring against the law of my mind, and bringing me into captivity to the law of sin which is in my members. O wretched man that I am! Who shall deliver me from the body of this death? (Rom. 7:15-24 KJV)

How can we be set free? The apostle Paul answers the question saying: "I thank God through Jesus Christ our Lord. So then with the mind I myself serve the law of God; but with the flesh the law of sin" (Rom. 7:25 KJV).

The root cause of the problem of man is selfishness—and selfishness which is being concerned with only oneself. It is seeking to satisfy the desires of the flesh. It is, also, the show of self, where self must be seen as more important and better above all others. It is seeking to be *first* and not the *last* in everything.

The problem of selfishness has its origin from the "I" idea of the angel, Lucifer, when he first sinned in Heaven. In Heaven Lucifer had desired to be like God, and he said to himself: "I will ascend into heaven; I will exalt my throne above the stars of God; I will also sit on the mount of the congregation on the farthest sides of the north; I will ascend above the heights of the clouds, I will be like the Most High" (Isa. 14:13-14 NKJV). This is the same idea by which the Serpent tempted Eve. He made her to think about what she could become in herself by aspiring to be like God if she ate of the tree of the knowledge of good and evil. Through this deception, Satan has led men to worship self instead of God.

Since Satan wants to rule in the lives of humans, he has also insinuated himself in the worship system of God. By the time Jesus came to this earth, Satan had taken control of the system of worship God gave to the children of Israel. That system of sacrificial services, devised by God to teach them the plan of salvation and to enable them to identify the Messiah, had only become a form without meaning.

It was the plan of God that Israel would be as heaven itself, *Zion the perfection of beauty,* and the center of worship here on earth, where the truth of God shines unto all other nations. The psalmist had said of Jerusalem, where the temple of God was erected: "Great is the Lord, and greatly to be praised in the city of our God, in the mountain of his holiness. Beautiful for situation, the joy of the whole earth, is Mount Zion, on the sides of the north, the city of the great King" (Ps. 48:1-2 KJV). "The mighty God, even the Lord, hath spoken, and called the earth, from the rising of the sun unto the going down thereof. Out of Zion, the perfection of beauty, God hath shined" (Ps. 50:1-2 KJV).

Israel had looked upon herself as the favored of God and was filled with pride. Instead of diffusing the light of the truth of God, she looked upon all other nations as inferior to herself and was not ready to have them share in the system of worship devised by God.

Filled with pride and looking for one who would break the yoke of the Roman Empire from her, Israel looked for a high and exalted Messiah. So in the first advent of Christ, the children of Israel failed to identify the Holy One of Israel, the meek and lowly Jesus. They had given themselves away to be deceived by Satan.

The Pharisees and scribes who professed to be the expositors of God's word became tools in the hands of Satan. Their lives were actuated by the spirit of Satan, and it was Satan making manifest his character of pride and selfishness through them.

Jesus, in an act to expose the work the enemy was working through the Pharisees and scribes, said to the Jews:

> The scribes and the Pharisees sit in Moses' seat: All therefore whatsoever they bid you observe, that observe and do; but do not ye after their works: for they say, and do not. But all their works they do for to be seen of men: they make broad their phylacteries, and enlarge the borders of their garments, and love the uppermost rooms at feasts, and the chief seats in the synagogues, and greetings in the markets, and to be called of men, Rabbi, Rabbi. (Matt. 23:2-7 KJV).

Jesus next taught the people and his disciples and said to them:

> But be not ye called Rabbi: for one is your Master, even Christ; and all ye are brethren. And call no man your father upon the earth: for one is your Father, which is in heaven. Neither be ye called masters: for one is your Master; even Christ. But he that is greatest among you shall be your servant. And whosoever shall exalt himself shall be abased; and he that shall humble himself shall be exalted. (Matt, 23:8-12 KJV)

The life of Jesus had been in a sharp contrast to the life of the Pharisees and scribes. His was a life of self-denial, theirs a life of self-exaltation. When the Pharisees and scribes sought to lord it over the people, Jesus came to serve. It was Jesus who said to his disciples: "The Son of Man did not come to be served, but to serve, and to give his life a ransom for many" (Matt. 20:28 NKJV).

The life of Jesus exposed the hypocrisy of the Pharisees and scribes, so they sought to kill him. As they were seeking to kill Jesus, it was Satan who, in seeking to hide the truth from man, sought to kill Jesus because the lives of the Pharisees and scribes reflected his character. In fact, it was Satan, who as a spirit being, was inhabiting the bodies of the Pharisees and scribes, manifesting himself before the people through them.

Just before his death, Jesus came to Caesarea Philippi with his disciples. Knowing he had but little time, he began to show, explicitly to the disciples, the end of his sacrificial ministry here on earth. The account of Matthew reads: "From that time Jesus began to show to his disciples that he must go to Jerusalem, and suffer many things from the elders and chief priests and scribes, and be killed, and be raised again the third day" (Matt. 16:21 KJV).

Peter could not accept that the Messiah would really be killed. Therefore he impetuously said to his Master: "Far be it from you, Lord; this shall not happen to you!" (Matt. 16:22 NKJV). But Jesus, knowing who had aroused Peter to speak, turned and said to Peter: "Get behind me, Satan! You are an offense to me, for you are not mindful of the things of God, but the things of men" (Matt. 16:23 NKJV).

Peter had unknowingly made himself an agent of Satan. Having no knowledge of God's salvation plan, he encouraged Jesus to escape suffering and death. But Jesus knew this was not the will of his Father. His life, as well as that of his followers, must be one of self-sacrifice, not one of self-gratification. Jesus then said to Peter and the rest of the disciples: "If anyone desires to come after me, let him deny himself, and take up his cross, and follow me. For whoever desires to save his life will lose it, and whoever loses his life for my sake will find it" (Matt. 16:24-25 NKJV).

As Christians, if we are to please God, we have to serve God with the spirit of self-sacrifice. Jesus, therefore, lists three things a Christian must be ready to do to be his follower. They are: deny himself, take up his cross, and follow him.

What does it mean to deny yourself? It means to surrender yourself completely, which means death to self. As the dead have died and surrendered their lives with their ambitions, pleasures, and desires, you willingly surrender your own ambitions, pleasures, and desires. In essence you give your whole life to God. It therefore means to relinquish ownership of yourself to God.

The person who has relinquished ownership of himself to God lives not to please self but to please God. His life is emptied of self and filled with the Holy Spirit, the power that overcomes sin and self. The apostle Paul wrote to the church at Corinth and said to them: "Or do you not know that your body is the temple of the Holy Spirit who is in you, whom you have from God, and you are not your own? For you were bought at a price; therefore glorify God in your body and in your spirit, which are God's" (1 Cor. 6:19-20 NKJV). Also testifying about the life of Jesus, the apostle, Paul, says: "For even Christ did not please himself; but as it is written, the reproaches of those who reproached you fell on me" (Rom. 15:3 NKJV).

Carrying a cross is a symbol of death. The Christian's life is a life of sacrificial service to God. It is to put to death your desires, that you may lose your old life, and live a new life of doing the will of God. But those who desire to preserve their own will and desires are not ready to put to death self; and for that matter, seek to save their own lives. If it were possible for them to preserve their lives for eternity, those who seek to preserve or keep safe their chosen lifestyles would do so. As they do not seek to put to death their old man of sin, in so doing they seek to save or preserve their lives of sin, if possible into life everlasting. But in the end, they will lose it. Thus said Jesus to his disciples: "If anyone desires to come after me, let him deny himself, and take up his cross, and follow me. For whoever desires to save his life will lose it, and whoever loses his life for my sake will find it" (Matt. 16:24-25 NKJV).

The last condition Jesus mentioned is that we follow him. To follow Jesus is to learn from him and be like him. It is to have the mental attitude of Jesus. Jesus made an appeal to his disciples, saying to them: "Take my yoke upon you and learn from me, for I am gentle and lowly in heart, and you will find rest for your souls" (Matt. 11:29 NKJV). The apostle, Paul, also tells us to cultivate the mental disposition of Jesus, saying:

> Let this mind be in you which was also in Christ Jesus, who, being in the form of God, did not consider it robbery to be equal with God, but made himself of no reputation, taking the form of a servant, and coming in the likeness of men. And being found in appearance as a man, he humbled himself and became obedient to the point of death, even the death of the cross. (Phil. 2:5-8 NKJV)

Jesus calls for Christians to be perfect. From the Sermon on the Mount, Jesus said to the people: "Be ye therefore perfect, even as your Father which is in heaven is perfect" (Matt. 5:48 KJV). The apostle Paul also tells us to be clothed with love, which is the bond or seal of perfection. He writes: "But above all these things put on love, which is the bond of perfection" (Col. 3:14 NKJV). Therefore, perfection in character is to be found in love. The apostle John testifies to this truth saying: "No man hath seen God at any time. If we love one another, God dwelleth in us, and his love is perfected in us" (1 John 4:12 KJV).

Jesus' call for us to be perfect like God is a call for us to be like God, who is love. To this end, the apostle John says:

> And we have known and believed the love that God hath to us. God is love; and he that dwelleth in love dwelleth in God, and God in him. Herein is our love made perfect, that we may have boldness in the day of judgment: because as he is, so are we in this world. (1 John 4:16-17 KJV)

The driving force which moves the spirit of self-sacrifice to work is love. Jesus, who is the personification of love, says:

> You shall love the Lord your God with all your heart, with all your soul, and with all your mind. This is the first and great commandment. And the second is like it: You shall love your neighbor as yourself. On these two commandments hang all the Law and the Prophets. (Matt. 22:37-40 NKJV)

One cannot be self-centered and, at the same time, obey these commands.

Submission to a life of self-sacrifice is not a distasteful course, but it is the secret to genuine joy and happiness. Happiness and joy are pivoted on love for God and love for our neighbors. Therefore, if we desire to be happy and radiate joy, we cannot do otherwise than to love God and our neighbors.

# THE WAY TO LOVE

The story is told of a rich young ruler who came to Jesus, seeking to know what he must do to inherit eternal life. The narrative reads:

> Now as he was going out on the road, one came running, knelt before him, and asked him, 'Good Teacher, what shall I do that I may inherit eternal life?' So Jesus said to him, 'Why do you call me good? No one is good but One, that is God. You know the commandments: Do not commit adultery, Do not murder, Do not steal, Do not bear false witness, Do not defraud, Honor your father and your mother.' And he answered and said to him, 'Teacher, all these I have observed from my youth.' Then Jesus, looking at him, loved him, and said to him, 'One thing you lack: Go your way, sell whatever you have and give to the poor, and you will have treasure in heaven; and come, take up the cross, and follow me.' But he was sad at this word and went away grieved, for he had great possessions. (Mark 10:17-22 NKJV)

What Jesus was asking the rich ruler to do was that he lay down his life (take up the cross) for his neighbors. Giving away his possessions would have meant death to himself, because it is the dead whose possessions are given to others; and the dead have no portion in the things of the earth. But this man would hold on to his possessions rather than lay down his life for his neighbors. He had the means to bring relief to those in need and suffering; but, because of his avarice, he would not.

The rich ruler had heaped riches unto himself. His heart was surcharged with greed for material wealth. Before Jesus he was revealed for who he really was. He did not love his fellow man as himself, because he was not ready to share his wealth with anybody. He showed himself to be a very selfish man. The life of the rich young ruler was in a marked contrast to the life of Jesus. In his death, Christ gave his life and all that he had for the rich ruler and all men. But this rich ruler was not willing to surrender all to Jesus.

The god of the young, rich ruler was not the God of love, but the god of mammon. He did not love God with all his heart and with all his soul and with all his mind and with all his strength. For when he was asked to sell all that he had and give to the poor that he might have treasure in heaven, he went away sorrowful. His desire was for the treasures of this earth, "where moth and rust destroy and where thieves break in and steal"; and not for the "treasures in heaven, where neither moth nor rust destroys and where thieves do not break in and steal" (Matt. 6:19-20 NKJV).

The root of all evil, the love of money, was planted in the heart of the rich ruler as a tree, and out of it flourished all evils. His was an outward form of righteousness; but in his heart he indulged in the pleasures of sin. He was as a "whitewashed tomb which indeed appear beautiful outwardly, but inside are full of dead men's bones and all uncleanness" (Matt. 23:27 NKJV).

The young, rich ruler was yet to know what the commandments he claimed to have kept from his youth meant. The apostle Paul, writing to the Romans, says:

> Owe no one anything except to love one another, for he who loves another has fulfilled the law. For the commandments, "You shall not commit adultery; you shall not murder; you shall not steal; you shall not bear false witness; you shall not covet; and if there is any

other commandment, are all summed up in this, saying, "You shall love your neighbor as yourself." Love does no harm to a neighbor; therefore, love is the fulfillment of the law (Rom. 3:8-10 NKJV).

The apostle, John, who wrote much about the love of God says: "Hereby *perceive* we the love of God, because he laid down his life for us" (1 John 3:16 KJV). Jesus also says: "Greater love has no one than this, than to lay down one's life for his friends" (John 15:13 NKJV). Love, which is charity and the love of God, simply means the giving of yourself and all that you have for your neighbor; and that is your life. This is why Jesus came to die for us; because of God's great love for a dying world, which stands in need of salvation. Therefore the Scripture says: "For God so loved the world that he gave his only begotten Son, that whoever believes in him should not perish but have everlasting life" (John 3:16 NKJV).

The apostle, John, who says that the perception of the love of God is to be found in his dying for us, also says that "God is love" (1 John 4:18 NKJV). In other words, the perception of love is to be found in death. This means the observation and identification of God is to be found in death, thus, his dying on the cross for our observation and identification of his person and character.

The way to love, therefore, is death. When we lay down our lives for our neighbors, we disown all that we have, because the dead have no portion in anything in the earth. So the apostle, Paul, says about Jesus: "For you know the grace of our Lord Jesus Christ, that though he was rich, yet for your sakes he became poor, that you through his poverty might become rich" (2 Cor. 8:9 NKJV).

If we are to be like Jesus, we are to emulate him. He gave his life for us, and we must be ready to give our lives for our neighbors. To this end the apostle John wrote:

> Hereby perceive we the love of God, because he laid down his life for us: and we ought to lay down our lives for the brethren. But whoso hath this world's good,

and seeth his brother have need, and shutteh up his bowels of compassion from him, how dwelleth the love of God in him? My little children, let us not love in word, neither in tongue; but in deed and in truth. (1 John 3:16-18 KJV)

The apostle Paul also says: "But do not forget to do good and to share, for with such sacrifices God is well pleased" (Heb. 13:16 NKJV).

# THE WAY TO LIFE

The way to life is death. Jesus, using natural objects to explain spiritual things, says: "Most assuredly, I say to you, unless a grain of wheat falls into the ground and dies, it remains alone; but if it dies, it produces much grain. He who loves his life will lose it, and he who hates his life in this world will keep it for eternal life" (John 12:24-25 NKJV).

Except we die to self, as a grain of wheat that falls into the ground and dies, we cannot enter eternal life. But if we die to self and bury our old lives in baptism, we enter into eternal life, and we bear the fruit of the Spirit of God.

The apostle Paul, writing to the churches of Galatia, admonished them saying:

> I say then: Walk in the Spirit, and you shall not fulfill the lust of the flesh. For the flesh lusts against the Spirit, and the Spirit against the flesh; and these are contrary to one another, so that you do not do the things that you wish. But if you are led by the Spirit, you are not under the law. Now the works of the flesh are evident, which are: adultery, fornication, uncleanness, licentiousness, idolatry, sorcery, hatred, contentions, jealousies, outbursts of wrath, selfish ambitions, dissensions, heresies, envy, murders, drunkenness, revelries, and the like; of which I tell you beforehand, just as I also

told you in time past, that those who practice such things will not inherit the Kingdom of God. But the fruit of the Spirit is love, joy, peace, long-suffering, kindness, goodness, faithfulness, gentleness, self-control. Against such there is no law. And those who are Christ's have crucified the flesh with its passions and desires. If we live in the Spirit, let us also walk in the Spirit. (Gal. 5:16-25 NKJV)

It is only when we crucify the flesh with its affections, which is dying to self, that we can bear the fruit of the Spirit. As we die to self, we become like seeds planted in the ground and to bear fruit.

When men die, before decomposition, their bodies become as hard as rocks; then they become numb to feeling. They lose their senses and nothing can penetrate their minds. The wise man, Solomon, says: "The dead know nothing" (Eccles 9:5 NKJV).

God, who made the heavens and the earth, lives as one who is dead. As the dead, God is like the rock—impenetrable. No evil can penetrate the mind of God. Moses says: "He is the Rock, his work is perfect; for all his ways are justice, a God of truth and without injustice; righteous and upright is He" (Deut. 32:4 NKJV). The psalmist also says: "For who is God, except the Lord? And who is a rock, except our God?" (Ps. 18:31 NKJV).

The dead are mindset. Nobody can change the frame of mind in which the dead died. If they died as righteous people, they are righteous forever; and if they died as wicked people, they are wicked forever. God, who lives as the dead, is mindset in righteousness, and nothing can change the mind of God. Jesus, who is God "manifest in the flesh," is that Rock which does not change. The scripture says: "Jesus Christ is the same yesterday, today, and forever" (Heb. 13:8 NKJV). If we are to be like God, we are to be like the dead who are mindset, and like God who is mindset in righteousness.

God is building a house in which to house His Spirit. This building is to be built with rocks, which are men who have died to self and, like God, have become mindset in righteousness. All who will live godly lives will together make up the building of God, which is to house the Spirit of God. The apostle, Paul, says:

> Now, therefore, you are no longer strangers and foreigners, but fellow citizens with the saints and members of the household of God, having been built on the foundation of the apostles and prophets, Jesus Christ Himself being the chief cornerstone, in whom the whole building, being joined together, grows into a holy temple in the Lord, in whom you also are being built together for a habitation of God in the Spirit. (Eph. 2:19-22 NKJV)

In the building of God, which is His sanctuary, every child of God is a lively stone, fit to be made a pillar, and Jesus the chief cornerstone. The apostle, Peter, in his epistle says:

You, also, as living stones, are being built up a spiritual house, a holy priesthood, to offer up spiritual sacrifices acceptable to God through Jesus Christ. Therefore, it is also contained in the Scripture, "Behold I lay in Zion a chief cornerstone, elect, precious, and he who believes in him will by no means be put to shame." (1 Peter 2:5-6 NKJV)

Jesus, also, in his revelation to the apostle John, says: "He who overcomes, I will make him a pillar in the temple of my God, and he shall go out no more" (Rev. 3:12 NKJV).

Those who will not do the will of God will be ground to powder by the body of Jesus, the Rock. When Jesus walked among men and the chief priests and elders and Pharisees rejected him, he told a parable and said to them: "Did you never read in the Scriptures: 'The stone which the builders rejected has become the chief cornerstone. This was the Lord's doing, and it is marvelous in our eyes'? ... And whoever falls on this stone will be broken; but on whomever it falls, it will grind him to powder" (Matt. 21:42-44 NKJV).

In the end of time, Jesus, who is the true Rock, will be that Rock which will destroy the wicked. The apostle John, in a vision prophesying the end time, says:

> And the kings of the earth, the great men, the rich men, the commanders, the mighty men, every slave and every free man, hid themselves in the caves and in the rocks of the mountains and said to the mountains and rocks, "Fall on us, and hide us from the face of him who sits on the throne and from the wrath of the Lamb! For the great day of his wrath has come, and who is able to stand?" (Rev. 6:15-17 NKJV)

Imagine Mount Everest, the highest mountain in the world, being lifted up and then dropped on you. How frightful that would be. But the day of the Lord will be more horrifying than that. The scripture says: "It is a fearful thing to fall into the hands of the Living God" Heb. 10:31 NKJV). The patriarch, Job, tells us that God hangs the earth on nothing. Job says: "He stretches out the north over empty space; he hangs the earth on nothing" (Job 26:7 NKJV). The apostle, Paul, also says: "And he (Christ) is before all things, and in him all things consist" (Col. 1:17 NKJV). This means everything is upheld by the hand of the Son of God. The earth, also, which weighs about 6.5 sextillion tons, is upheld by the hand of the Son of God. The human mind cannot fathom with what power God upholds the universe. And if the universe is upheld by the hand of our Lord and Savior, Jesus Christ, how fearful it will be for those who reject him who is the Spiritual Rock and who has reared the earth and its mountain ranges and in whose hands all these things are upheld.

# THE WAY TO PEACE

Of all the created beings on earth, it is only man whom God has endowed with the powers of conscience and memory. This is so because God made man in his likeness, with the ability to choose to love and to hate. Unlike man the animals behave instinctively. For example, a lion can kill a man and not feel worried about its actions, because it does not have any conscience, and it is just its nature to behave so.

Man's ability to reason, coupled with his power of conscience, has serious implications. It implies that man has to be responsible for his actions. His bad choices in his dealings bring to him a conscience of guilt, while his good choices give to him a sense of joy and satisfaction.

Since the inception of sin, the sense of guilt feelings has been on the human race. But our way of escape has been provided by the blood of Jesus Christ. The apostle, Paul, speaking about the work Christ performed on behalf of man when he went to the cross, says of him:

> And, having made peace through the blood of his cross, by him to reconcile all things unto himself; by him, I say, whether they be things in earth, or things in heaven. And you, that were sometime alienated and enemies in your mind by wicked works, yet now hath he reconciled in the body of his flesh through death, to present you holy and unblameable and unreproveable in his sight. (Col. 1:20-22 KJV)

One of the greatest weapons of Satan against men is the sense of guilt feelings. It is the work of the enemy to bring to our memory the knowledge of our past sins, and thereby to make us have guilt feelings. As long as we have guilt, we have no peace with God.

If we are to enter into the peace of God, we have to die to the knowledge of our sins, after we have confessed of them. For the dead have entered into peace and rest. We must see ourselves like those who are dead and buried in the grave with all our sins. For even the very wicked of the earth, who lived their lives by perpetrating wickedness, in their death carry with them their work of wickedness.

It is through death that God forgives our sins and takes away the remembrance of our sins from his presence. This is why the blood of Christ cleanses us from all sin. The Scripture says: "And according to the law almost all things are purged with blood, and without shedding of blood there is no remission" (Heb. 9:22 NKJV). As we confess our sins and plead for the forgiveness of sins, Christ looks to his death and forgives and forgets our sins as though we have never sinned. As the dead do not have knowledge of anything, in his death, Christ does not see our sins.

To the end that we may be like Christ, who lived a perfect life and who, in his death, does not see our sins, the apostle Paul wrote, saying:

> Or do you not know that as many of us as were baptized into Christ Jesus were baptized into his death? Therefore we were buried with him through baptism into death, that just as Christ was raised from the dead by the glory of the Father, even so we also should walk in newness of life. For if we have been united together in the likeness of his death, certainly we also shall be in the likeness of his resurrection, knowing this, that our old man was crucified with him, that the body of sin might be done away with, that we should no longer be slaves of sin. For he who has died has been freed from sin. Now if we died with Christ, we believe that we shall also live with him...For

the death that he died, he died to sin once for all; but the life that he lives, he lives to God. Likewise you also, reckon yourselves to be dead indeed to sin, but alive to God in Christ Jesus our Lord. (Rom. 6:3-11 NKJV)

# THE WAY TO THE CHARACTER OF GOD

The way to the character of God is to be found in death. In death the spirit of the dead, of even those who are boisterous, are made quiet. And God, who lives as one who is dead, has a quiet Spirit. The mouths of the dead are stopped from talking, and those who want to be like God must learn to be quiet. If the dead could hear, all they would do is listen to the living speak, because, in order to listen, we must be quiet; and the dead are quiet. Thus James in his epistle says: "Therefore, my beloved brethren, let every man be swift to hear, slow to speak" (James 1:19 NKJV).

In death there is a perfect keeping of the commandments of God. The murderer ceases from killing, and the thief ceases from stealing. The fornicator yields his passions, and the talebearer's lips are sealed. The covetous man, also, gives up his desires and becomes content with his estate, which is lying naked in the grave. In the end, every man ceases from his works and enters into rest.

The beauty of the character of God, which is in a quiet and gentle spirit, is to be found in death. The apostle Peter, giving counsel to married women, but advice which pertains also to every child of God, says:

> Likewise you wives, be submissive to your own husbands, that even if some do not obey the word, they, without a word, may be won by the conduct of their wives, when they observe your chaste conduct accompanied by fear. Do not let your beauty be that outward adorning of arranging the hair, of wearing gold, or of putting on

fine apparel; but let it be the hidden person of the
heart, with the incorruptible ornament of a gentle and
quiet spirit, which is very precious in the sight of God.
(1 Peter 3:1-4 NKJV)

The treasure of God is in a quiet spirit which signifies a good character. Solomon says: "A good name is to be chosen rather than great riches, loving favor rather than silver and gold" (Prov. 22:1 NKJV). And again Solomon says: "A good name is better than precious ointment, and the day of death than the day of one's birth" Eccles. 7:1 NKJV).

The beauty of the character of God is likened to gold, and silver, and precious stones, which are embedded in rocks. Although gold and silver are precious, the character of God who is the true Rock surpasses these in splendor. The psalmist says:

> The law of the Lord is perfect, converting the soul the
> testimony of the Lord is sure, making wise the simple;
> the statutes of the Lord are right, rejoicing the heart;
> the commandment of the Lord is pure, enlightening
> the eyes; the fear of the Lord is clean, enduring forever;
> the judgments of the Lord are true and righteous
> altogether. More to be desired are they than gold, yea,
> than much fine gold; sweeter also than honey and the
> honeycomb. (Ps. 19:7-10 NKJV)

Again the psalmist says: "The law of your mouth is better to me than thousands of shekels of gold and silver" (Ps. 119:72 NKJV).

In the journey of the children of Israel from Egypt to Canaan, God told them to make him a sanctuary. "Then the Lord spoke to Moses, saying: 'Speak to the children of Israel, that they bring me an offering. From everyone who gives it willingly in his heart you shall take my offering. And let them make me a sanctuary, that I may dwell among them" (Exod. 25:1, 2, 8 NKJV).

In the earthly sanctuary erected in the wilderness, there was to be a high priest and other priests to minister in its services. God said to

Moses: "Now take Aaron your brother, and his sons with him, from among the children of Israel, that he may minister to me as priest, Aaron and Aaron's sons: Nadab, Abihu, Eleazar, and Ithamar" (Exod. 28:1 NKJV).

The attire of the high priest and the other priests ministering in the sanctuary were to be holy garments designed by God himself. The Lord said to Moses:

> And you shall make holy garments for Aaron your brother, for glory and for beauty. And these are the garments which they shall make: a breastplate, an ephod, a robe, a skillfully woven tunic, a turban, and a sash. So they shall make holy garments for Aaron your brother and his sons that he may minister to me as priest.
>
> They shall take the gold and blue and purple and scarlet thread, and fine linen, and they shall make the ephod of gold and blue and purple and scarlet thread, and fine linen thread, artistically woven... And the intricately woven band of the ephod, which is on it, shall be of the same workmanship, woven of gold and blue and purple and scarlet thread, and fine linen thread. Then you shall take two onyx stones and engrave on them the names of the sons of Israel. Six of their names on one stone, and the remaining six names on the other stone, according to their birth. With the work of an engraver in stone, like the engravings of a signet, you shall engrave the two stones with the names of the sons of Israel. You shall set them in settings of gold. And you shall put the two stones on the shoulders of the ephod as memorial stones for the sons of Israel. So Aaron shall bear their names before the Lord on his two shoulders as a memorial...

You shall make the breastplate of judgment. Artistically woven according to the workmanship of the ephod you shall make it: of gold and blue and purple and scarlet thread, and of fine linen thread, you shall make it... And you shall put settings of stones in it, four rows of stones: The first row shall be a sardius, a topaz, and an emerald; this shall be the first row; the second row shall be a turquoise, a sapphire, and a diamond; the third row, a jacinth, an agate, and an amethyst; and the fourth row, a beryl, an onyx, and a jasper. They shall be set in gold settings. And the stones shall have the names of the sons of Israel, twelve according to their names, like the engravings of a signet, each one with its own name; they shall be according to the twelve tribes. (Exod. 28:2-21 NKJV)

As the high priest was to minister in the holy place before the Lord, and as he bore the names of the children of Israel in precious stones, it was to signify that the high priest was presenting the children of Israel as precious in the Lord's sight. And when the Lord made himself manifest in the Most Holy place, and saw the breastplate on the high priest, with the names of the children of Israel engraved in the precious stones in the breastplate, he saw the children of Israel as precious in his sight.

It is the will of God to make his children as precious as gold and silver and precious stones, and even to cover them with precious stones, like those Lucifer was covered with when he was a holy angel in heaven. God, describing Lucifer as he was in heaven, says about him: "You were in Eden, the garden of God; every precious stone was your covering: the sardius, topaz, the diamond, beryl, onyx, and jasper, sapphire, turquoise, and emerald with gold" (Ezek. 28:13 NKJV). And God speaking through the prophet Isaiah as to how he will make man, says: "I will make man more precious than fine gold; even a man than the golden wedge of ophir" (Isa. 13:12 KJV).

The apostle John, in a vision, was made to behold the New Jerusalem, the holy city, which symbolizes the children of God. Describing what he saw, John says:

> Then one of the seven angels who had the seven bowls filled with the seven last plagues came to me and talked with me, saying, 'Come I will show you the bride, the Lamb's wife.' And he carried me away in the Spirit to a great and high mountain, and showed me the great city, the holy Jerusalem, descending out of heaven from God, having the glory of God. And her light was like a most precious stone, like a jasper stone, clear as crystal. Also she had a great and high wall with twelve gates, and twelve angels at the gates, and names written on them, which are the names of the twelve tribes of the children of Israel... And the construction of its wall was of jasper; and the city was pure gold, like clear glass. And the foundations of the wall of the city were adorned with all kinds of precious stones: the first foundation was jasper, the second sapphire, the third chalcedony, the fourth emerald, the fifth sardonyx, the sixth sardius, the seventh chrysolite, the eighth beryl, the ninth topaz, the tenth chrysoprase, the eleventh jacinth, and the twelfth amethyst. And the twelve gates were twelve pearls: each individual gate was of one pearl. And the street of the city was pure gold, like transparent glass. (Rev. 21:9-21 NKJV)

# HUMILITY:
# THE PRECIOUS PEARL OF GOD

The science of the Cross of Calvary is the greatest discovery that can ever be made by every man. It is the greatest treasure to be found in a lost world. Finding this treasure is to find the pearl of great price. So Jesus says:

> The kingdom of heaven is like treasure hidden in a field, which a man found and hid; and for joy over it he goes and sells all that he has and buys that field. Again, the kingdom of heaven is like a merchant seeking beautiful pearls; who, when he had found one pearl of great price, went and sold all that he had and bought it. (Matt. 13:44-46 NKJV)

The apostle Paul wrote to the Christians at Corinth and said to them': "For I determined not to know anything among you except Jesus Christ and him crucified" (I Cor. 2:2 NKJV).

> It is the promise of God to give to His children His treasures. As those who seek the treasures of gold and precious stones mine rocks for their treasure, so those who search the scriptures diligently, like miners who search for hidden treasure in rocks, will be rewarded with the treasures of God, who is the True Rock, which we are to mine for His hidden treasures. For thus says the Lord: "I will give you the treasures of darkness and

hidden riches of secret places, that you may know that I, the Lord, who call you by your name, am the God of Israel" (Isa. 45:3 NKJV).

The wise are clothed with humility. The apostle Peter counsels the children of God to be clothed in such manner. He says: "Likewise you younger people submit yourselves to your elders. Yes, all of you be submissive to one another, and be clothed with humility, for God resists the proud, but gives grace to the humble" (1 Peter 5:5 NKJV).

The way to humility is death. In death every man is humbled. The proud are brought low in death; and the master is brought down from his golden bed to be made equal with the servant as they make their bed together in the grave. The rich are also brought to poverty; and the prince is made a pauper, as they lose their wealth and princely robes in death. In the grave, fools, also, become wise and the wicked become loving. For in death, they cease from their foolish and wicked deeds. The patriarch, Job, speaking about death, says, "There the wicked cease from troubling, and there the weary are at rest. There the prisoners rest together; they do not hear the voice of the oppressor. The small and great are there and the servant is free from his master" (Job 3:17-19 NKJV)

Those who desire to be like God, go by the way of learning to be like God; and that way is to have a taste of death. Learning to be like God who is the Rock, is to become like the Rock, that you may hide in you the treasures you possess from Him, to beautify your rock.

Jesus, revealing the hidden treasures of heaven to his disciples, said to them: "If anyone desires to come after me, let him deny himself, and take up his cross and follow me. For whoever desires to save his life will lose it, and whoever loses his life for my sake will find it" (Matt. 16:24-25 NKJV). Jesus repeated this doctrine to the Pharisees in other words, saying to them: "For whoever exalts himself will be abased, and he who humbles himself will be exalted" (Luke 14:11 NKJV).

It is the living who are exalted, for they stand tall, but the dead lie low, leveled with the ground. If we are to learn to humble ourselves, we must be like the dead who lie low and are hidden in the ground. The dead do not seek to be exalted; neither do they seek to be known, and being dead they are hidden from the view of the living.

Rocks are symbols of the dead. The very first treasure and property of rocks, is that they are inanimate. In other words, they are like the dead, without life. Another quality of rocks is that they are unchangeable in nature. Strong clouds may rise, the winds may blow, and the storms may come, but the rocks remain the same; unchangeable. Such is the character of God. Thus, it is written about Him: "He is the Rock, his work is perfect: for all his ways are judgment: a God of truth and without iniquity, just and right is he." (Deut. 32:4 KJV)

When Jesus spoke to the children of Israel, teaching them how to be a true disciple of his, he could see among them some who would not choose to be like him. Thus, he said to them: Assuredly, I say to you, there are some standing here who shall not taste death till they see the Son of Man coming in his Kingdom" (Matt. 16:28 NKJV) Those who do not taste of death now will taste death when time shall be ushered into eternity.

Death is the school of God, where we learn to be like God. And in the end, every intelligent being will enter the school of God, one way or the other. We either choose to enter in by surrendering ourselves to God and to die to self, or wait for the last day when God shall come and make all those who have been their own gods through self-worship to enter the school of death. The *last day* on earth, will be God's way of teaching those who have been their own gods the correct way to be like God.

Lucifer had said in Heaven, "I will be like the Most High" (Isa. 14:14 KJV). Later when he, as Satan and the Serpent, tempted Eve in the Garden of Eden, he told her if she should eat of the tree of the knowledge of good and evil, she would not surely die, but her eyes would be opened, and she would be like God. But that was a deception. So Jesus, who is God come in the flesh, came to the earth and died, and in his death showed to the universe how to be like God.

In the end of time, the destruction of Lucifer will not be an arbitrary act of God, but an answer to the desire of Lucifer. Lucifer, now Satan, and all those who never learned the way of humility will lie in the grave, and they will be humbled forever. Lucifer had desired to be like God, and God will make him to be like God, when he will be humbled forever. God dwells in humility; and since Lucifer had desired to be like God, through eternal ages, he will lie still in humility, when he shall enter into death and go the way of learning to be like God. And it takes eternity to be like God.

It was self-exaltation that led to the fall of Lucifer. God speaking about the fall and end of Lucifer says:

> How you are fallen from heaven, O Lucifer, son of the morning! How you are cut down to the ground, you who weakened the nations! For you have said in your heart: I will ascend into heaven, I will exalt my throne above the stars of God; I will also sit on the mount of the congregation on the farthest sides of the north; I will ascend above the heights of the clouds, I will be like the Most High. Yet you shall be brought down to sheol, to the lowest depths of the Pit. Those who see you will gaze at you, and consider you, saying: Is this the man who made the earth tremble, who shook kingdoms, who made the world as a wilderness and destroyed its cities, who did not open the house of his prisoners? ... But you are cast out of your grave as an abominable branch, like the garment of those who are slain, thrust through with a sword, who go down to the stones of the pit, like a corpse trodden underfoot. (Isa 14:12-19 NKJV)

Still speaking through the prophet Isaiah about the end of Lucifer, God says:

> Hell from beneath is excited about you, to meet you at your coming; it stirs up the dead for you, all the chief ones of the earth; it has raised up from their thrones

all the kings of the nations. They shall speak and say to you: Have you also become as weak as we? Have you become like us? Your pomp is brought down to sheol, and the sound of your stringed instruments; the maggot is spread under you, and worms cover you. (Isa. 14:9-11 NKJV)

Lucifer had desired to be the *first* and the greatest, and to set his throne equal to the throne of God; but, in the end, he shall be the least in all of God's created beings.

Until, as Christians, we learn to be the *last* in everything, we shall never attain to perfection. Why? Because when the wealth of the world is distributed among men, the dead have no portion in anything. The wise man, Solomon, says: "The dead know nothing, and they have no more reward ... nevermore will they have a share in anything done under the sun" (Eccles.9:5-6 NKJV).

If we should have our mental disposition as that of the dead, we shall not seek to have any portion of the things of the earth, and we will not covet anything. For the dead have no ambition, neither do they have any desire for anything. They are content with their estate, which is lying naked in the grave.

The reason Adam and Eve were naked before they sinned is that, in their perfect state, they were as the dead. When Job was tempted by Satan and after he had lost all his possessions, he said: "Naked I came from my mother's womb, and naked shall I return there" (Job 1:21 NKJV). The apostle Paul, warning Christians against covetousness, says: "But godliness with contentment, is great gain. For we brought nothing into this world, and it is certain we can carry nothing out. And having food and clothing, with these we shall be content" (1 Tim. 6:6-7 NKJV).

Just before Jesus began his ministry on earth, he went to the River Jordan to be baptized of John. As John saw Jesus coming, he said to the people who had gathered at the River Jordan, "Behold! The Lamb of God who takes away the sin of the world" (John 1:29 NKJV). Earlier the Jews had sent priests and Levites from Jerusalem to ask John whether he was the Christ or Elijah or the Prophet who was to come. When John confessed he was not the Christ, they asked him, saying: "Why then do you baptize if you are not the Christ, nor Elijah, nor the Prophet?" John answered them, saying: "I baptize with water, but there stands one among you whom you do not know. It is he who, coming after me, is preferred before me, whose sandal strap am not worthy to lose" (John 1:24-25 NKJV). It appears Jesus must have hid himself in the crowd, as John spoke about him. The people also must have looked around to see who it was John spoke about; but they could not find him. It is not the nature of Jesus to make a display of himself; but rather it is his nature to act as the dead in all things. As Jesus might have hidden himself, he was like the dead who are hidden in the grave from the sight of the living.

Those who seek perfection in character will never seek to be seen or known among men as important or to be highly esteemed. Rather those who seek to be perfect, humble themselves before every man. They see others as much better than themselves because they live as though they are dead. The apostle, Paul, writing to the disciples at Philippi, said to them: "Let nothing be done through selfish ambition or conceit, but in lowliness of mind let each esteem others better than himself" (Phil. 2:3 NKJV).

# THE WAY TO PATIENCE

It has been said when the feathers are unruffled everybody can be a Christian. But when the feathers are ruffled, will all the professed disciples of Christ stand true to the test of patience?

It is only when the bird is dead that it will not feel threatened or peck when its feathers are ruffled. It is then that you can run your fingers several times through its feathers, and it will lie still in perfect peace. Having the mental disposition of the dead is the secret to patience. It is what guards against rashness, and harshness, and retaliation.

The story is told of a pastor who was visiting a church in another town, and as he was trying to follow the directions to the church, he drove abruptly in front of another car. The driver of the car changed lanes and drove next to the pastor's car, cursed the pastor, and drove on. Upon arrival at the church and to the surprise of the pastor, he saw the man who had cursed him. The man also realized the person he had cursed on the road was the visiting pastor, as he, as an elder of the church, was being introduced by the resident pastor. Ashamed the elder did not know what to do.

Another story is told of a man who worked as a courier and was always in a hurry on his errands. The faster he worked, the more money he made, because he could then pick up more business. So he would always blow his horn, telling everybody to move out of his way. One day as he was driving his van and, as usual, was blowing his horn, he came to a traffic light. The light was red, so he stopped. But when the light changed to green for him to go, he was not moving, so the cars behind him began blowing their horns at him. Later when a policeman came to find out what had happened to the man, he found him slumped over his steering wheel. The emergency medical service was called, and on arrival they pronounced the man dead. He had died of heart failure.

The dead are in no hurry to go anywhere. They move only after others move them. They wait for others to take them to church for a funeral service and to the cemetery for burial. They are never impatient when the living delay. They never lose time for they are ever present as dead; and being dead, they are content with their estate, which is lying quietly in their graves.

To the dead, a thousand years and a day are the same; and they never age. Just as a day comes to pass them, so, also, a thousand years come to pass, and they remain the same—dead. The man who has been dead a thousand years and the man who has been dead just a day are the same. Being dead they do not know the fleeting of time. The day and the night are the same to them, and nothing changes for them. The apostle Peter speaks about the ever-present God, the one who lives as though he is dead, saying: "But beloved, do not forget this one thing, that with the Lord one day is as a thousand years, and a thousand years as one day" (2 Pet. 3:8 NKJV).

God is eternal, and the day in which He dwells is also eternal. Eternity is one day which never ends. There is no tomorrow for the dead, and there is no night in the eternity of God.

At the end of his earthly ministry, Jesus stood as one who was dead before his accusers and the governor, Pontius Pilate. He was falsely accused, unjustly tried, disgraced, afflicted, and sentenced to death. But through it all, he was so calm, so serene, and so at peace; because living as though he were dead, he possessed the calmness and serenity of the dead. As the dead, he could not be moved to retaliate.

The prophet Isaiah, prophesying about the suffering and death of Jesus, said: "He was oppressed and he was afflicted, yet he opened not his mouth; he was led as a lamb to the slaughter, and as a sheep before its shearers is silent, so he opened not his mouth" (Isa.53:7 NKJV). And on the night before Jesus was crucified, it is said of him: while he was being accused by the chief priests and elders, he answered nothing. Then Pilate said to him, 'Do you not hear how many things they testify against you?' And he answered him not one word, so that the governor marveled greatly" (Matt. 27:12-14 NKJV).

The dead are defenseless. And those who seek for perfection in character will not seek to defend themselves when falsely accused or treated despitefully. Jesus, in the Sermon on the Mount, said to his disciples:

> You have heard that it was said, "An eye for an eye and a tooth for a tooth" But I tell you not to resist an evil person. But whoever slaps you on your right cheek, turn the other to him also. If anyone wants to sue you and take away your tunic, let him have your cloak also. And whoever compels you to go one mile, go with him two. Give to him who asks you, and from him who wants to borrow from you do not turn away. (Matt. 5:38-42 NKJV).

> The apostle, Peter, admonishing Christians to be like Jesus said:

> For to this you were called, because Christ also suffered for us, leaving us an example, that you should follow his steps: Who committed no sin, nor was guile found in his mouth; who when he was reviled, did not revile in return; when he suffered, he did not threaten, but committed himself to him who judges righteously; who himself bore our sins in his own body on the tree, that

we, having died to sins, might live for righteousness—
by whose stripes you were healed. (1 Pet.2:21-24
NKJV)

# THE VOCATION OF THE PERFECT LIFE

Of all the vocations in life, the one which brings the greatest honor, though it appears to be the least, is the work of a servant. Service to God and man, expressed in love, is to be much desired among those who seek perfection in character.

When the apostles James and John came to Jesus, desiring that one sit on his right hand and the other on his left when he is come in his glory, there arose a contention among the twelve apostles as to who should be the greatest. But knowing their thoughts, Jesus called them to himself and said to them:

> You know that those who are considered rulers over the Gentiles lord it over them, and their great ones exercise authority over them. Yet it shall not be so among you; but whoever desires to become great among you shall be your servant. And whoever of you desires to be first shall be slave of all. For even the Son of Man did not come to be served, but to serve, and to give his life a ransom for many. (Mark 10:42-45 NKJV)

Luke, recording the same incident, says:

> Then a dispute arose among them as to which of them would be greatest. And Jesus, perceiving the thought of their heart, took a little child and set him by him, and said to them, Whoever receives this little child in my name receives me; and whoever receives me

receives him who sent me. For he who is least among you all will be great. (Luke 9:46-48 NKJV)

Those who perform the work of servants are like the dead. In service to their masters and their fellow men, they do not question the nature of their duties or how they are to be performed. They just do as they are bidden. When men die, they are carried where others will take them. For example, the dead are taken to the cemetery by others, and they do not open their mouths against those who take them there. In other words, the dead go where they are asked to go. And this, is the nature of the work of a servant.

Servants offer themselves in sacrifice to serve; and by serving, they perform the humblest job. Jesus, the servant to all mankind, who came to give his life as a ransom for the sins of men, on his last Passover feast with his disciples, stooped down and served them by performing the work which was the work of slaves in those days. The record of it reads:

> "Now before the feast of the Passover, when Jesus knew that his hour had come that he should depart from this world to the Father, having loved his own who were in the world, he loved them to the end. And supper being ended, the devil having already put it into the heart of Judas Iscariot, Simon's son, to betray him, Jesus, knowing that the Father had given all things into his hands, and that he had come from God and was going to God, rose from supper and laid aside his garments, took a towel and girded himself. After that, he poured water into a basin and began to wash the disciples' feet, and to wipe them with the towel with which he was girded... So when he had washed their feet, taken his garments, and sat down again, he said to them, 'Do you know what I have done to you? You call me Teacher and Lord, and you say well, for so I am. If I then, your Lord and Teacher, have washed your feet, you also ought to wash one another's feet. For I have given you an example, that you should do

as I have done to you. Most assuredly, I say to you, a servant is not greater than his master; nor is he who is sent greater than he who sent him. If you know these things, happy are you if you do them. (John 13:1-7 NKJV)

Servants give. As the dead, whose possessions are given to others, servants give of the possessions entrusted to them, to serve others. As I was making a study into this aspect of the perfect life, I had in my possession things I had discontinued to use. I took them and gave them away.

We live in a world where many have lots of money hoarded in banks—money which could go to invest in other people's lives, to those in need—just sit in banks, while others suffer. If we are going to live happy and fulfilled lives, we have to serve others with our possessions, as God who has given to us all good things. The psalmist says of the great Life giver:

> O Lord, how manifold are your works! In wisdom you have made them all. The earth is full of your possessions—This great and wide sea, in which are innumerable teeming things, living things both small and great... These all wait for you, that you may give them their food in due season. What you give them they gather in; you open your hand, they are filled with good. (Ps. 104:24-28 NKJV).

The result of giving is reception. This means the way to receive is to give. When we stop giving, nobody receives.

All the operations of nature are based on the conformity to the law of love, the law of giving. For example, during the process of photosynthesis, plants use carbon dioxide to prepare their food, and release oxygen, an important element for the survival of man, into the atmosphere. The carbon dioxide plants need to prepare their food is also released by man and animals in the process of respiration.

If man should destroy all vegetation, he would eventually destroy himself, because there would be no plants to release the oxygen, which man needs to survive; and the whole atmosphere would be filled with carbon dioxide. Likewise, if all animal life should be destroyed, plants would eventually die, because there would be no carbon dioxide for them to prepare their foods.

The rain cycle on the face of the earth also operates on the law of giving. The tributaries of rivers give their water to the mainstream rivers, and the mainstream rivers in turn give the water they receive to the sea. The sea then, through evaporation, gives the water it receives to the atmospheric heavens; and the atmospheric heavens, through condensation, give the water received back to the rivers. And the cycle goes on. The wise man Solomon says: "All the rivers run into the sea, yet the sea is not full; to the place from which the rivers come, there they return again" (Eccles. 1:7 NKJV). But if perchance the sea should not give the water it receives to the atmospheric heavens, the atmospheric heavens would not have any water to give to the tributaries. The tributaries also would not have any water to give to the mainstream rivers and would dry up. The mainstream rivers, also, not having any water coming in from the tributaries, would dry up and will not have any water to give to the sea. Eventually the sea would also dry up. The sea, through selfishness, would have destroyed itself.

Our most important duty as servants of God, while salvation lasts, is to serve our neighbors by sharing the gospel with them. True servants of God share the gospel, so others may know the truth. It is their delight to bring life to the perishing. The Prophet, Isaiah, says about those who bear the message of salvation: "How beautiful upon the mountains are the feet of him who brings good news, who proclaims peace, who brings glad tidings of good things, who proclaims salvation, who says to Zion, 'Your God reigns!'" (Isa. 52:7 NKJV). The wise man, Solomon, also says: "The generous soul will be made rich, and he who waters will also be watered himself" (Prov. 11:25 NKJV).

If we should fail in our duty to deliver the gospel, in the end, the sea of the multitude of people of this world will be destroyed, and we will be destroyed along with them, because we failed to give to them, the water of life.

God warns us against the consequences of failing to warn the world of the coming doom. His warning comes to us through the prophet, Ezekiel, saying:

> Son of man, I have made you a watchman for the house of Israel; therefore hear a word from my mouth, and give them warning from me: When I say to the wicked, 'You shall surely die,' and you give him no warning, nor speak to warn the wicked from his wicked way, to save his life, that same wicked man shall die in his iniquity; but his blood I will require at your hand. Yet, if you warn the wicked, and he does not turn from his wickedness, nor from his wicked way, he shall die in his iniquity; but you have delivered your soul. (Ezek. 3:17-19 NKJV)

The reason so many Christians fail to share the gospel is because we have not organized our time. We do not set specific time aside to go to our neighbors and to share the gospel with them. So even though we may have it on our minds to share the gospel, because we have not made up our minds when to go, we are at a standstill.

If you are going to share the gospel with your neighbors, you will need to have a defined time in your busy schedule to go to your neighbors and, as a servant and messenger of God, deliver to them the good news of salvation. We are to work like couriers who work by delivering mail and packages. Those we cannot reach by regular visits, we are to write them, sending them Christian literature to read. Such was the nature of the work of the apostles as they wrote the epistles. Also in this regard, we are to set specific time aside to write to our loved ones. For example, I have personally set aside Sunday from two o'clock in the afternoon to about six o'clock in the evening to visit with my neighbors. During this time I am about the work of the Master. I make appointments with people I know and visit with them at the time appointed. I begin with just visiting to see their welfare and to converse with them about things in general. This leads my neighbors and loved ones to confide in me the burdens of their hearts. I often look out for needs which I can fulfill, and so, on my next visit, I can take with me some gift to satisfy a need, or a small gift as a token of my love. This is to win the confidence and affection of my neighbors. It also opens the door for sharing the gospel. I may then at a later visit leave with them some literature to read and ask to have Bible studies with them.

It is very important we develop very personal, intimate relationships with our neighbors, so that they will know we love them. It is only then we can successfully share with them the good news of the gospel. The apostle Paul admonishes us saying: "By love serve one another" (Gal. 5:13 KJV).

# THE WAY TO DESTROY THE DEVIL AND HIS WORKS

There is a way to destroy the devil and his works, and that way is death. There are three things which war against man. They are Satan, Sin, and Self. But as stated earlier, the greatest of these three is Self. God, speaking about what led to the fall of Lucifer, says:

> You were the anointed cherub who covers; I established you; you were on the holy mountain of God; you walked back and forth in the midst of fiery stones. You were perfect in your ways from the day you were created, till iniquity was found in you... Your heart was lifted up because of your beauty; you corrupted your wisdom for the sake of your splendor. (Ezek.: 28.14-17 NKJV)

It is evident it is self which led to the fall of Lucifer. He had looked at the beauty of himself and was filled with pride.

All the evils committed in the world have been committed by the man called self. A man angry for his pride being wounded will kill his brother, because self is very much alive in him. People will fight over the least misunderstanding because self, lives in them. Nations will go to war when they cannot have their way, because the lives of their leaders are inhabited by self. A man will covet what belongs to another and will desire to have it, regardless, because self, dwells in him. A man will steal from his neighbor, because, by his actions, he implies that he has need of those things he steals more than his neighbor. By stealing the thief also implies his neighbor is dead, and he must have his possessions; because the dead have no portion in the things of the earth. A man will dishonor his father and mother and those who are his elders, because to him, the counsel of every man is foolishness and he is the only wise man. The wise man, Solomon, says: "The way of a fool is right in his own eyes, but he who heeds counsel is wise" (Prov. 12:15 NKJV)

The apostle, Paul, describing the conditions that will be prevalent on the earth towards the end of time says:

> But know this that in the last days perilous times will come: For men will be lovers of themselves, lovers of money, boasters, proud, blasphemers, disobedient to parents, unthankful, unholy, unloving, unforgiving, slanderers, without self-control, brutal, despisers of good, traitors, headstrong, haughty, lovers of pleasure rather than lovers of God. (2 Tim. 3:1-4 NKJV)

Because self-love will be on the rise, the love for our neighbors will wax cold in many. This explains why there will be wars and rumors of wars in the end of time. Because Satan will be ripening self in men, men will kill at the slightest injury.

The battleground of the spiritual warfare, between the spirit of self and the spirit of self-denial in the life of every man, is the mind. Our thoughts expressed in our actions, are a manifestation of which spirit is working in our lives. God has his weapons for us in this warfare. The apostle Paul comments on the weapons of God, saying:

> For though we walk in the flesh, we do not war according to the flesh. For the weapons of our warfare are not carnal but mighty in God for pulling down strongholds, casting down arguments and every high thing that exalts itself against the knowledge of God, bringing every thought into captivity to the obedience of Christ. (2 Cor. 10:3-5 NKJV)

If we are to win the battle against Satan and sin, we have to destroy self in us. The apostle, Peter, therefore tells us that, since Jesus suffered and died for us, Christians are to arm themselves as soldiers with the spirit and mental attitude that worked in Jesus. He writes:

> For Christ also suffered once for sins, the just for the unjust, that he might bring us to God, being put to death in the flesh but made alive by the Spirit... Therefore, since Christ suffered (died) for us in the flesh, arm yourselves with the same mind, for he who has suffered (died) in the flesh has ceased from sin, that he no longer should live the rest of his time in the flesh for the lusts of men, but for the will of God. (1 Pet. 3:18; 4:1-2 NKJV)

As soldiers of the cross, our awareness to combat every temptation is death. We are to meet every temptation by saying to ourselves, "I am dead." If we should condition our minds to be in the state of the dead, Satan can never take us unawares with temptation. In fact it is impossible to tempt the dead with sin, because being dead they have no desire for anything.

Unless we reach the state in which Satan cannot tempt us with sin, though he will present it to us, we cannot attain to perfection. And that state which we should reach to attain perfection is death. When men die, they are placed beyond the power of the tempter, and he cannot have power over them again. So when, in our minds, we enter into death, the tempter has no power over us, and sin is powerless over us. So says the scripture: "For he who has died has been freed from sin" (Rom. 6:7 NKJV). Therefore, the way to destroy the devil and his works is death.

One of the reasons why Jesus came into the world to die was to destroy the devil. The epistle to the Hebrews, believed to have been written by the apostle Paul, speaking about the death of Jesus, says:

> But we see Jesus, who was made a little lower than the angels, for the suffering of death crowned with glory

and honor, that he, by the grace of God, might taste death for everyone. For it was fitting for him, for whom are all things, in bringing many sons to glory, to make the author of their salvation perfect through sufferings... Inasmuch then as the children have partaken of flesh and blood, he himself likewise shared in the same, that through death he might destroy him who had the power of death, that is, the devil, and release those who through fear of death were all their lifetime subject to bondage. (Heb. 2:9-15 NKJV)

# WHY SUFFERING

The question of why God allows suffering has been perplexing both to believers and non-believers. Non-believers' question that if God is good and all-loving, why does he allow suffering to come upon men. Believers also just cannot understand why God allows all kinds of suffering to come upon them.

There are two basic kinds of suffering. One of them is not hard to explain. It is that kind of suffering which we bring upon ourselves because of our sins, weaknesses and shortcomings. God allows us to suffer the consequences of our actions so that we may see the results of our sins. The other kind of suffering which has been difficult to explain is that kind of suffering which the children of God are called upon to suffer for righteousness sake. This is the kind of suffering you suffer not because you sinned but because you serve God. So then why does God allow this kind of suffering?

In the controversy between good and evil, Satan contends that evil is more powerful than righteousness, and in the face of suffering righteousness is flawed. This contention was manifested when Satan went before God and had a dialogue with God about Job. God had used Job as his showcase of perfection in character amidst evil. Testifying about the perfect character of Job, God said to Satan, "Have you considered my servant Job that there is none like him on the earth; a blameless and upright man, one who fears God and shuns evil?" (Job 1:8 NKJV) But Satan countered God and said, "Does Job fear God for nothing? Have you not made a hedge around him, around his household, and around all that he has on every side? You have blessed the work of his hands and his possessions have increased in the land. But now, stretch out your hand and touch all that he has, and he will surely curse you to your face!" (Job1:9-11 NKJV) So the Lord said to Satan, "Behold, all that he has is in your power, only do not lay a hand on his person." (Job 1:12 NKJV)

Satan, by saying that, "But now, stretch out your hand and touch all that he has, and he will surely curse you to your face," inferred that if God should allow suffering to come upon Job, Job's perfect character will fall apart in the face of suffering, and he will embrace evil by cursing God. Thus, Satan contends that in the face of suffering, righteousness and holiness falls apart. In other words, by analyzing and rephrasing what Satan said, should read, "There is a weakness in righteousness and holiness through suffering." So, in all the sufferings that Satan brought upon Job, it was his attempt to prove that in the face of sufferings a just and upright person falters and compromises with evil.

In his contention with God about the perfect character of Job, Satan implied that people can only be perfect in good times and when the goodness of the Lord is upon them, but when evil is come nobody can be perfect. The challenge thrown to God by Satan was about perfection in character in the face of evil and suffering. Thus, Satan's contention about the perfect character of Job was a question mark he placed on the perfect character of God.

It is God who claims to be perfect. The sublime argument of Satan therefore by inference was that God had claimed to be perfect when there was no evil, but since his inception of evil, God cannot claim to be perfect unless he has lived through the sufferings of evil and he should still maintain his integrity. As he spoke with God, Satan did not speak in clear direct speech, because he does not want the children of men to know and understand what he is doing to them.

Satan had conquered the earth with evil and he boasted intimating that nobody can come to the earth and not succumb to the power of evil. So, he made his case against the perfect character of Job, which was the character of God. It was God living out his perfect character in his obedient servant Job, through the power of the Holy Spirit. And if nobody can dwell on the earth and not succumb to the power of evil through sufferings, that will include God, and that will make evil more powerful than righteousness. So, the argument of Satan about the perfect character of Job was indirectly about the perfect character of God. However, Satan was to first prove his case against Job and later against God when he lowered himself to be a man.

The argument and challenge of Satan called for God to come to the earth to vindicate his character or for Satan to prove that indeed evil is more powerful than righteousness. So, God had to become a man in the person of Jesus Christ to face evil and to be tested with suffering. Therefore, one of the main reasons why Jesus came to the earth was to vindicate the character of God. In the process of vindicating the character of God, he was to save those who had fallen under the power of evil and show them how to live victoriously over the power of Satan. To this end the scripture declares about Jesus saying:

> But we see Jesus, who was made a little lower than the angels for the suffering of death, crowned with glory and honor; that he by the grace of God should taste death for every man. For it became him, for whom are all things, and by whom are all things, in bringing many sons unto glory, to make the captain of their salvation perfect through sufferings. (Heb. 2:9-10 KJV)

The contention of Satan that God cannot claim to be perfect because his claim to perfection was before evil existed is the reason why Jesus had to suffer to prove that he is perfect always, and as the scripture says, "To make him perfect through sufferings." So, God was manifested in the flesh and he was tempted with the sufferings of evil in every way as men suffer but he came out victorious over every form of suffering. He has therefore obtained the title, "The Holy One of Israel." (Isa. 54:5, KJV) Since he suffered like men suffer, he is touched with their feelings. The scripture therefore says of him, "For we have not an high priest which cannot be touched with the feeling of our infirmities; but was in all points tempted like as we are, yet without sin." (Heb. 4:15 KJV)

The writer of the book of Hebrews continue to say about Jesus, saying: "Though he were a Son, yet learned he obedience by the things which he suffered. And being made perfect, he became the author of eternal salvation unto all them that obey him." (Hebrews 5:8-9 KJV)

In this contest thrown to God by Satan, God was made a spectacle unto both men and angels as he was tested with suffering. The entire universe watched to see whether the charge brought against God by Satan was true or if God would vindicate his character. Since God, in the person of Jesus triumphed over every test of suffering, therefore the scripture declares about him saying: "And without controversy great is the mystery of godliness: God was manifest in the flesh, *justified* in the Spirit, *seen* of angels, preached unto the Gentiles, believed on in the world, received up into glory." (1 Tim. 3:16 KJV)

In all the sufferings Satan brought to bear on Jesus, it was his attempt to bring the Creator under his power and control. But to the dismay of Satan and his host of evil angels, God in the person of Jesus triumphed over every test of suffering they brought upon him. On the cross when Jesus declared, "It is finished," the verdict on the charges of Satan was concluded as false and God's character was vindicated before the whole universe. God made an open show throughout his life of suffering that the charges brought against him by Satan were all false as he triumphed over every form of suffering. On the cross the contest came to an end and the victory of God was sealed with his death. The apostle Paul therefore says about the defeat of Satan and the victory of Jesus: "And having spoiled principalities and powers, he made a shew of them openly, triumphing over them in it." (Col. 2:15, KJV)

The conflict which Satan began in heaven and was later transferred to the earth, was about who will have the supremacy to rule the universe. Since Satan could not get the rule over the universe through reasoning, he decided to get it through the power of force. So, Satan contends that evil is more powerful than righteousness. If evil is more powerful than righteousness, then Satan will have to prove it by bringing the Creator under the power of evil. And if Satan can bring the Creator to submit to the power of evil, then the Creator and his whole creation will become subject to Satan, and he will mount the throne as God to rule over the universe.

This is to make us understand why God came to the earth in the form of man, to the territory where Satan has conquered every child born of a woman, so that God could be subjected to the powers of evil.

However, if Satan was able to accomplish his assumption to bring the Creator to submit to the powers of evil, then in the end this king of fools would have destroyed the Source of Life and the whole creation. The Creator would have died never to rise again, and the whole universe with its teeming creatures, including Satan himself, also would have died, never to rise again.

Also, if Jesus had submitted to the powers of evil, it would have meant that God the Father, God the Son and God the Holy Spirit sinned, because it is in the body of Jesus that, "dwells all the fulness of the Godhead bodily." (Colossians 2:9 KJV) Again, if Jesus had compromised with evil, the holy angels of heaven, who have not sinned, would have had their spirits contaminated with evil, because it is the Spirit of Christ, the Source of Life, which like electric current flows to indwell them, giving them life and making them holy.

What Lucifer did not know to understand, though he will fight against it, is that the law of God is the source of life; and that is what God is—the Law! When a rich young ruler came to Jesus and asked him, saying, "What must I do to inherit eternal life?" Jesus answered, saying: "If thou wilt enter into life, keep the commandments. (Matt. 19:17, KJV)

It is by keeping the commandments of God, that both angels and men will receive eternal life. The law of God as the source of life is what generates eternal life. If the law is destroyed, all life-forms will be destroyed, including God, and there will be no more life.

Since the law cannot be destroyed, the Apostle John declares about God and says: "This then is the message which we have heard of him, and declare unto you, that God is light, and in him is no darkness at all." (1 John 1:5, KJV) The wise man Solomon also says: "For the commandment is a lamp; and the law is light." (Proverbs 6:23, KJV)

The law, which is light and the source of life, is personified in God. When you see God, you have seen the law which is light. The Law is that Word of God which is God. The scriptures say: "The law is light," and "God is Light."

Jesus is He who is that Word which is God and Light. Therefore, if Jesus who is God and Light was to have sinned, the law which is light would have died in Him, and God would have entered darkness and eternal death, never to rise again. So, all those who reject the law of God, which is the source of life and the light of life, will in the end have destroyed themselves. They will fall into darkness and die eternally.

So, therefore, the day is coming, when Satan, the king of fools, who seeks to rule the universe with sin, will die, never to rise again. The word of God speaks about the end of Satan and the angels who followed in his folly, saying: "And the angels which kept not their first estate, but left their own habitation, he hath reserved in everlasting chains under darkness unto the judgment of the great day." (Jude verse 6 KJV)

Thus, all sinners who die in their sins, in them the vision of the universe is destroyed. The vision of the universe is destroyed in sinners because if they were entrusted with the stewardship of the universe, they sinned and destroyed the source of life, the law, from giving life to the universe. This explains the reason why since Adam and Eve sinned, there is death and decay in the earth.

The authority God gave to Adam and Eve, to have dominion over the earth, implied that by their obedience to the law, the source of life would emanate through them to sustain the life of all living things on the earth. But when they sinned, the Source of Life, the Law, was withdrawn from them and from the earth.

Since the source of life, the law, was withdrawn from the earth because of Adam and Eve's sin, it has been replaced with lawlessness and the result has been death, with the children of the earth practicing the things that leads to death. Animals have also been affected, with some becoming wild beast destroying life, because the law, the source and sustainer of life has been removed from the earth. So, this part of the universe which was entrusted to man has become the valley of death.

It is only the grace of God which has given the earth and its inhabitants hope in restoration through the blood of the Son of God. Everyone who believes will be restored, but those who reject the grace of God, reject the source of life, to their own peril.

Since the contest between good and evil focuses on the character of God, and the contention of Satan is that, the character of God is flawed in the face of suffering, it therefore calls for every follower of Jesus to suffer like he suffered. Jesus therefore warns every one of his disciples saying:

> If the world hate you, ye know that it hated me before it hated you. If ye were of the world, the world would love his own: but because ye are not of the world, but I have chosen you out of the world, therefore the world hateth you. Remember the word that I said unto you. The servant is not greater than his Lord. If they have persecuted me, they will also persecute you: If they have kept my saying; they will keep yours also. But all these things will they do unto you for my name's sake, because they know not him that sent me. (John 15:18-21 KJV)

The apostle Paul also puts every Christian on the alert saying: "Yea, and all that will live godly in Christ Jesus shall suffer persecution." (2 Tim. 3:12 KJV)

As God allowed Satan to test his servant Job with suffering, so he will allow Satan to test every one of his children. The question to be settled by every Christian is, "Am I going to succumb to evil and live under the power of evil when suffering comes or am I going to maintain mine integrity?"

The character of God must be vindicated in every child of God. It must be proven in every follower of Christ that he or she stands firm and rooted in righteousness both in good times and in bad times.

One of the deadliest sins in the face of suffering is the feeling of bitterness which leads to the sin of murmuring. It was with the sin of bitterness by which Satan sought to destroy John the Baptist. When John languished in prison, tempted with the sin of bitterness, Satan led him to doubt if Jesus was the Messiah. And John who had declared Jesus as the "Lamb of God," wavered in his faith. John had sent his disciples to inquire of Jesus asking him, "Art thou he that should come, or do we look for another?" (Matt. 11:3 KJV) But Jesus sent the disciples of John back to John with the message saying, "…Blessed is he, whosoever shall not be offended in me." (Matt. 11:6 KJV)

If John the Baptist thought languishing in prison was something bad that happened to him, the worst was yet to happen to him. In the end, Satan working through Herodias and her daughter had John the Baptist beheaded. The scriptures therefore warn the children of God of the feeling of bitterness saying, "Looking diligently lest any man fail of the grace of God; lest any root of bitterness springing up trouble you, and thereby many be defiled." (Heb. 12:15 KJV)

When you maintain your integrity in the face of suffering, you become like the man in the parable of Jesus, who built his house upon a rock. The storms of suffering may beat upon you, but you will stand firm grounded in the Rock. But if you should succumb to evil when suffering comes then you will be like the man who built his house on sand. The storms of suffering will come and great will be your fall. This would mean that you have not fortified yourself in the Spiritual Rock.

We can only be fortified in Christ who is the Spiritual Rock with his word abiding in us to gain the victory. The apostle Paul therefore encourages us saying, "But thanks be to God, which giveth us the victory through our Lord Jesus Christ. Therefore, my beloved brethren, be ye steadfast, unmovable, always abounding in the work of the Lord, forasmuch as ye know that your labor is not in vain in the Lord." (1Cor. 15:57-58 KJV)

The will of God in the lives of his children is that his perfect character be manifested in them in times of adversity as well as in good times. We are to be like him, who is, "the same yesterday, today and forever." To this end, James admonishes the children of God saying, "My brethren count it all joy when ye fall into diverse temptations; knowing this, that the trying of your faith worketh patience. But let patience have her perfect work, that ye may be perfect and entire, wanting nothing." (James 1:2-4 KJV)

Those who would go through suffering for the cause of God and to be victorious over Satan and his charges shall inherit the kingdom of God. Jesus therefore in the beatitudes pronounces blessings on those who suffer for righteousness sake saying, "Blessed are they which are persecuted for righteousness sake for theirs is the kingdom of heaven. Blessed are ye when men shall revile you and persecute you and shall say all manner of evil against you falsely for my sake: Rejoice, and be exceeding glad: for great is your reward in heaven: for so persecuted they the prophets which were before you." (Matt.5:10-12 KJV)

Since the great controversy between good and evil is centered on whether the character of God is perfect or not in the face of suffering, we honor God when we go through suffering and come out as overcomers. This has led the inspired writer Ellen White, to comment saying: "Of all the gifts that Heaven can bestow upon men, fellowship with Christ in His sufferings is the weightiest trust and the highest honor." (Desire of Ages, p. 225)

Those who are called upon to suffer are like Job, honored by God, and by suffering and overcoming they honor God. They honor God because by standing firm and maintaining their integrity in the face of the trials of suffering, they prove the charges of Satan to be false. So did Job honor God. After all the sufferings Satan brought to bear on Job, he declared by saying, "though he (God) slays me yet will I trust him." (Job 13:15, KJV)

The apostle Peter therefore encourages the children of God to rather rejoice when they are tested with all manner of trials as they are being made partakers in the sufferings of Christ that they may also be partakers in his glory. Peter writes saying: "Beloved, think it not strange concerning the fiery trial which is to try you, as though some strange thing happened unto you: But rejoice, inasmuch as ye are partakers of Christ's sufferings; that, when his glory shall be revealed, ye may be glad also with exceeding joy. If ye be reproached for the name of Christ, happy are ye; for the spirit of glory and of God resteth upon you: on their part he is evil spoken of, but on your part he is glorified." (1 Pet. 4:12-14, KJV)

In this contest between good and evil, the children of God like their master are made a spectacle unto men and angels. Men and angels are to be witnesses to see if the professed children of God will allow the character of God to be vindicated in them. Christ the Captain of our salvation has been victorious over Satan and sin. He has set the example for every child of God to follow. Therefore, we are exhorted to follow his example. The exhortation in the epistle to the Hebrews says:

> Wherefore seeing we also are compassed about with so great a cloud of witnesses, let us lay aside every weight, and the sin which doth so easily beset us, and let us run with patience the race that is set before us. Looking unto Jesus the author and finisher of our faith, who for the joy that was set before him endured the cross, despising the shame, and is set down at the right hand of the throne of God. For consider him that endured such contradiction of sinners against himself, lest ye be wearied and faint in your minds. (Heb. 12:1-3 KJV)

The questions which every child of God should find answers to are: "How did Jesus overcome every temptation and suffering of evil and how shall we endure temptation and suffering like Jesus?" The secret to Jesus's perfect life is that in all his life, he lived as one who was dead to sin but alive unto righteousness, which is the principle of baptism. His mental disposition was as one who was dead to sin and the suffering of evil. Like the dead who cannot be aroused to sin nor suffer the pain of affliction, Jesus lived inanimate to sin or suffering. His life was one of self-denial which is living with the mind-set of death.

The suffering and death of Jesus on the cross was to demonstrate how God lives. In all the sufferings that Satan brought to bear on Jesus, he responded as one who was dead. Living as the dead he could not be aroused to retaliate to do any evil. Thus, it is said of Jesus who set an example for us to follow when he suffered on the cross:

For even hereunto were ye called: because Christ also suffered for us, leaving us an example, that ye should follow his steps: Who did no sin, neither was guile found in his mouth: who when he was reviled, reviled not again; when he suffered, he threatened not; but committed himself to him that judgeth righteously: Who his own self bare our sins in his own body on the tree, that we, being dead to sins, should live unto righteousness: by whose stripes ye were healed. (1 Pet. 2:21-24 KJV)

If as children of God we should be overcomers over evil like Jesus did, we must follow his example and live like he lived. We must be armed against evil with the weapon Jesus used to overcome evil and suffering. And that weapon is death, which is the essence of baptism; to die to sin.

The children of God are to live by the principle of being baptized daily; which is daily dying to sin but alive unto righteousness. The apostle Peter therefore counsels us saying: "Forasmuch then as Christ hath suffered (died) for us in the flesh, arm yourselves likewise with the same mind: for he that hath suffered (died) in the flesh hath ceased from sin: That he no longer should live the rest of his time in the flesh to the lusts of men, but to the will of God." (1 Pet. 4:1-2 KJV) The apostle Peter is encouraging us to arm ourselves with the weapon of death as the dead cannot be aroused to the lust of the flesh, neither can they be inflicted with pain nor to suffer injury.

Like rocks which are without life and impregnable, the dead are without life and their minds are impregnable to sin, suffering or anything else. In like manner, Jesus who is the Spiritual Rock, living as one who is dead to sin, has his mind impregnable to sin and suffering. Therefore, if we are to be overcomers like Jesus, we are to be like rocks which are inanimate and impregnable; and then fortify ourselves in the Spiritual Rock who is inanimate to sin and suffering.

Our refuge from the assault of sin and suffering is to be found in the Spiritual Rock, which is Christ. We are to be like Moses who God hid in the rock when God revealed his glory to him. The psalmist says: "He that dwelleth in the secret place of the Most high shall abide under the shadow of the Almighty. I will say of the LORD, He is my refuge and my fortress: my God; in him will I trust." (Psalm. 91:1-2, KJV)

How can we then endure suffering? If we should look at the dead, they have suffered the ultimate of suffering. In the state of death, the dead have lost everything, but they lie still in quietude. The dead are destitute of everything, but they do not suffer from want; neither can the dead feel to suffer the pain of affliction. In the state of death, the dead cannot see to be intimidated with fear or to have a fear of what could happen in the future. They do not fret for losing time, nor do they worry about anything. Also, the dead cannot hear to suffer from the pain of humiliation and insults. These are the principles of self-denial and dying to self.

The virtue of patience which we should exemplify throughout all our sufferings can only be obtained as we practice the silence of the dead by the power of the Spirit of God. This is how Jesus lived and in this lies the beauty of the holy character of God, which should be our adornment. Thus, the apostle Peter in his epistle advising husbands and wives on what God reckons as beautiful adornment says: "Whose adorning let it not be that outward adorning of plaiting the hair, and of wearing of gold, or of putting on of apparel: But let it be the hidden man of the heart, in that which is not corruptible, even the ornament of a meek and quiet spirit, which is in the sight of God of great price." (1 Pet. 3:3-4 KJV)

We are counseled to follow the example of the patience of Job, the prophets and of the Lord Jesus Christ. James the brother of Jesus says: "Take my brethren, the prophets, who have spoken in the name of the Lord, for an example of suffering affliction, and of patience: Behold, we count them happy which endure. Ye have heard of the patience of Job, and have seen the end of the Lord; that the Lord is very pitiful, and of tender mercy." (James 5:10-11, KJV) Again, James counsels the children of God to endure temptation and suffering, saying: "Blessed is the man who endures temptation; for when he has been approved, he will receive the crown of life which the Lord has promised to those who love Him." (James 1:12, NKJV)

The writer of the book of Hebrews, speaks about the affliction and persecution that some who had faith in God suffered. He says: "Others were tortured, not accepting deliverance, that they might obtain a better resurrection. Still others had trial of mockings and scourgings, yes, and of chains and imprisonment. They were stoned, they were sawn in two, were tempted, were slain with the sword. They wandered about in sheepskins and goatskins, being destitute, afflicted, tormented—of whom the world was not worthy. They wandered in deserts and mountains, in dens and caves of the earth." (Hebrews 11:35-38, NKJV)

Also speaking about the sufferings of Moses, the Hebrews writer says: "By faith Moses, when he became of age, refused to be called the son of Pharaoh's daughter, choosing rather to suffer affliction with the people of God than to enjoy the passing pleasures of sin, esteeming the reproach of Christ greater riches than the treasures in Egypt; for he looked to the reward. By faith he forsook Egypt, not fearing the wrath of the king; for he endured as seeing Him who is invisible. (Hebrews 11:24-27, NKJV)

In the end, it will be said of those who would have suffered for righteousness sake and still maintain their integrity: "Here is the patience of the saints: here are they that keep the commandments of God, and the faith of Jesus." (Rev. 14:12 KJV) The patience of the saints is their endurance through trials which is found in their dying to sin and suffering. Their endurance through suffering is like gold which shines brightly when tested with fire.

Like the dead, we must be diligently dead to sin. The wise man Solomon says: "Keep thy heart with all diligence; for out of it are the issues of life." (Prov. 4:23 KJV) The diligence by which we are to keep our hearts from sin, is death. The dead are diligently dead. Nothing can change the estate of the dead nor do they seek to do anything else besides being dead.

Our awareness and to be on the alert like well-prepared soldiers to do battle when sin and evil approaches in whatever form, is death. We are to fortify the defenses to our senses with the mighty weapon of death. When sin and evil encroach on us whether by sight, imagination, hearing, feel or touch, taste and smell, if we should have our minds fortified with the mental disposition of the dead, they will be powerless over us.

We are to defeat evil with these three words: "I am dead," and the great "I AM" will empower us with his Holy Spirit to gain the victory. Having this knowledge, the apostle Paul says: "I am crucified with Christ: nevertheless I live; yet not I, but Christ liveth in me: and the life which I now live in the flesh I live by the faith of the Son of God, who loved me, and gave himself for me." (Gal. 2:20, KJV)

Jesus promises to bestow his honor on those who will overcome the testing of suffering, like he overcame. He says: "To him that overcometh will I grant to sit with me in my throne, even as I also overcame, and I am set down with my Father in his throne." (Rev. 3:21, KJV) In a vision, the apostle John was made to hear how God blesses those who die to sin and suffering. He says: "And I heard a voice from heaven saying unto me, write. 'Blessed are the dead which die in the Lord from henceforth: Yea, saith the Spirit, that they may rest from their labors: and their works follow them." (Rev. 14:13 KJV)

The contest between good and evil on earth is coming to an end. Since Satan claims that the suffering of evil is more powerful than righteousness, the day is coming, when God will bring such suffering of his righteous indignation against evil and its perpetrators and it will be very tempestuous. Satan and his host will be made to suffer the wrath of God to see if they will be able to endure it. It will be as if God is saying to Satan, "Enjoy suffering which you claim to be more powerful than righteousness."

God will make Satan to be a spectacle unto men and angels that they may see if Satan will endure and be found laughing in the sufferings that God will bring on him, when God shall cast him into the lake of fire. But those who would endure suffering in affliction, tribulation and persecution because of the charges Satan has cast on the character of God, upon them will God bestow his glory. To this end the apostle Paul writes these comforting words, saying:

> We are bound to thank God always for you, brethren, as it is fitting, because your faith grows exceedingly, and the love of every one of you all abounds toward each other, so that we ourselves boast of you among the churches of God for your patience and faith in all your persecutions and tribulations that you endure, which is manifest evidence of the righteous judgment of God, for which you also suffer, since it is a righteous thing with God to repay with tribulation those who trouble you, and to give you who are troubled rest with us when the Lord Jesus is revealed from heaven with his mighty angels, in flaming fire taking vengeance on those who do not know God, and on those who do not obey the gospel of our Lord Jesus Christ. These shall be punished with everlasting destruction from the presence of the Lord and from the glory of his power, when he comes, in that day, to be glorified in his saints and to be admired among all those who believe, because our testimony among you was believed. (2 Thess. 1:3-10 NKJV)

Speaking about the reward that shall be manifested in the saints of God, the apostle Paul, says: "For I consider that the sufferings of this present time are not worthy to be compared with the glory which shall be revealed in us." (Rom. 8:18 NKJV) Paul also wrote to the church at Corinth and said to them: "For our light affliction, which is but for a moment, is working for us a far more exceeding and eternal weight of glory, while we do not look at the things which are seen, but at the things which are not seen. For the things which are seen are temporary, but the things which are not seen are eternal." (2 Cor. 4:17-18 NKJV)

Therefore, all those who are suffering for the cause of God, should take to heart the counsel of the apostle Peter, where he says:

"Be sober, be vigilant; because your adversary the devil walks about like a roaring lion, seeking whom he may devour. Resist him, steadfast in the faith, knowing that the same sufferings are experienced by your brotherhood in the world. But may the God of all grace, who called us to His eternal glory by Christ Jesus, after you have suffered a while, perfect, establish, strengthen, and settle you. To Him be the glory and the dominion forever and ever. Amen." (1 Pet. 5:8-11 NKJV)

To those who will live by this secret to perfect living, which is the secret to the perfect life of Jesus, the apostle Paul declares the promises of God, saying: "It is a faithful saying: For if we be dead with him, we shall also live with him: If we suffer, we shall also reign with him…" (2 Tim. 2:11-12 KJV)

# GOD'S SIGN TO PERFECT LIVING

God has a sign to his peace and rest, and this sign, which is the way to living a perfect life, is spelled out in the Ten Commandments. Because this law is God's sign and way to living a perfect life, Satan seeks to destroy it from the minds of men. Even Christendom, which should uphold the law of God, claims that out of the Ten Commandments, the Fourth Commandment, the law which calls men to the rest of God, was given only to the Jews, and, therefore may be disregarded. It is true the Ten Commandments were given to the Jews. But the question is: Who is a Jew? The apostle Paul says: "For he is not a Jew who is one outwardly, nor that circumcision which is outward in the flesh; but he is a Jew who is one inwardly, and circumcision is that of the heart, in the Spirit, and not in the letter; whose praise is not from men but from God" (Rom. 2:28-29 NKJV). In other words, he is not a Jew who is born one in the flesh; but he is a Jew who is born again in the heart by the Spirit of God; and to him is the law of God given.

The Fourth Commandment reads:

> Remember the Sabbath day, to keep it holy. Six days you shall labor and do all your work, but the seventh day is the Sabbath of the Lord your God. In it you shall do no work: you, nor your son, nor your daughter, nor your manservant, nor your maidservant, nor your cattle, nor your stranger who is within your gates. For in six days the Lord made the heavens and the earth, the sea and all that is in them, and rested the

> seventh day. Therefore, the Lord blessed the Sabbath
> day and hallowed it. (Exod. 20:8-11 NKJV)

God named the days of the week by numbers. It is men who have named the days of the week after the planetary system and Anglo-Saxon gods. God has named the days of the week by numbers because as a memorial of the creation, he would have us to know what he did specifically on each day and especially for us to know which day is the Sabbath. So in the creation account it is expressed what God did in each of the days of the week. Also, in the fourth Commandment, it is clearly stated which day is the Sabbath and evidently why the seventh day is the Sabbath. The fourth Commandment, therefore, is a summary of the creation account, and the creation account in the book of Genesis, is also an elaboration of the Fourth Commandment.

Everything that God has made is to be a study for us. In them are the lessons and principles which he will have us to gain the knowledge of his glory. God made the Sabbath day, the seventh and last day of the week specifically for *rest* and no *work*. In the first six days of creation, God worked in those days. But the seventh day was void of work.

The principle in the Sabbath day which God would have us to learn is to be as the dead. It is only the living who work. The dead have ceased from their work and have entered into rest; and therefore, the Fourth Commandment, God's way to living a perfect life, which calls us to cease from our works, calls us to enter into death. Thus, on the Sabbath day, God calls us to cease from our works and enter into his rest, as the dead who have ceased from their works and have entered into rest. As we do this, we cease from the toils and burdens of this life, which steal from us our peace of mind.

Moreover, when men die, the day on which they die is their *last* day on earth, and it ends their *work*, and they enter *rest*. Likewise the Sabbath, the *last* of the days of the week, in which God calls us to bring to an *end* our *work*, is a call for us to enter into *death* and *rest* like those who have entered into their *last* day by dying and have entered into *rest*.

Therefore, the Sabbath day, as the day in which we are to set aside our work and be as the dead who do not work, is the science of death and as such the science of the death of Jesus. Thus, the fourth commandment, the Sabbath law, is the science of the cross.

Just before God delivered the children of Israel from slavery in Egypt, he gave them a message of deliverance through the prophet Moses. In the message, the children of Israel were to have blood of slain lambs on the doorposts of their houses. The scripture says:

> Now the Lord spoke to Moses and Aaron in 'the land of Egypt, saying..."speak to all the congregation of Israel, saying: 'On the tenth day of this month every man shall take for himself a lamb, according to the house of his father, a lamb for a household...Your lamb shall be without blemish, a male of the first year. You may take it from the sheep or from the goats. Now you shall keep it until the fourteenth day of the same month. Then the whole assembly of the congregation of Israel shall kill it at twilight. And they shall take some of the blood and put it on the two doorposts and on the lintel of the houses where they eat it. Then they shall eat the flesh on that night; roasted in fire, with unleavened bread and with bitter herbs they shall eat it... And thus you shall eat it: with a belt on your wrist, your sandals on your feet, and your staff in your hand. So you shall eat it in haste. It is the Lord's Passover... Now the blood shall be a sign for you on the houses where you are. And when I see the blood, I will pass over you; and the plague shall not be on you to destroy you when I strike the land of Egypt." (Exod. 12: 1-13 NKJV)

On the day, the children of Israel were delivered from Egypt, they *rested* from the toil of slavery. That day was their *last* day as slaves in Egypt, and it *ended* their *work* as slaves in Egypt. As the dead who *ended* their *work* on their *last day* and entered into *rest*, the children of

Israel *ended* their *work* on their *last day* as slaves and entered into *rest*, and the Lord gave to them his commandment saying:

> Observe the Sabbath day, to keep it holy, as the Lord your God commanded you. Six days you shall labor and do all your work, but the seventh day is the Sabbath of the Lord your God. In it you shall not do any work: you, nor your son, nor your daughter, nor your manservant, nor your maidservant, nor your ox, nor your donkey, nor any of your cattle, nor your stranger who is within your gates, that your manservant and your maidservant may rest as well as you. And remember that you were a slave in the land of Egypt, and that the Lord your God brought you out from there by a mighty hand and by an outstretched arm; therefore the Lord your God commanded you to keep the Sabbath day. (Deut. 5:12-15 NKJV)

> In the same manner as God gave the Sabbath commandment as a memorial, when he ended his work of creation on the seventh day and rested, he also gave the Sabbath commandment to the children of Israel as a memorial when their work as slaves in Egypt came to an end.

The deliverance of the children of Israel from Egyptian slavery was to symbolize the deliverance of God's people from the slavery of sin. Also, the blood on the doorposts was to symbolize the application of the death and blood of the Lamb of God to the hearts and minds of God's people. The apostle, Paul, speaking on the deliverance from sin, says:

> Do you not know that to whom you present yourselves slaves to obey, you are the one's slaves whom you obey, whether of sin to death, or of obedience to righteousness? But God be thanked that though you were slaves of sin, yet you obeyed from the heart that

form of doctrine to which you were delivered. And having been set free from sin, you became slaves of righteousness. (Rom. 6:16-18 NKJV)

The children of God are to live their lives as those who are *dead* and have *ended* their *work* of sin. Having *died* to sin, they have been set free to be no more a people who live their lives in bondage to do the work of sin, but to be alive unto righteousness. Therefore, the apostle Paul says: "Knowing this, that our old man was crucified with Him, that the body of sin might be done away with, that we should no longer be slaves of sin. For he who has *died has* been freed from sin." (Rom. 6:6-7 NKJV)

If the children of God are to live their lives like those who are *dead*, then every day of their lives is to be like their *last* day; like the dead who entered their *last* day on the day they *died*. Therefore, the children of God are to live every day by the principle of the seventh and *last* day of the week, the day of *rest* that they may *rest* from the *works* of sin.

Jesus pleads with sinners saying to them: "Come to me, all you who *labor* and are heavy laden, and I will give you *rest*" (Matt. 11:28 NKJV). This plea of Jesus, is an invitation for sinners to come to him and to bring to an *end* their *work* of sin; that they may live as the *dead* who have *died* and have *ended* their *work* and entered into *rest*.

When we disobey God to walk in our own ways, the path we choose is one of affliction, *labor* and hardship. This is because, it is only God who has the best answer to every need. Every other way is an awkward way and must be done in hardship.

To choose to observe the Sabbath is to choose to obey God in everything. It is choosing to do the will of God which brings the best result in every human need and takes away the problem of hardship, which we bring upon ourselves in choosing to do our own ways, This is the essence of the Sabbath law; to *rest* from our *labors*.

In his purposes and in his word, God uses the number seven to denote completion and perfection. There are the seven stars, the seven churches, the seven trumpets, the seven seals and the seven last plagues, all in the book of Revelation, and the seventh of every one of them brings to completion a purpose of God. Also, God created the heavens, the earth and the things in them in six days and rested the seventh day, bringing his work of creation to completion. The bible account of the end of the creation says:

> Thus, the heavens and the earth, and all the host of them, were finished. And on the seventh day God ended his work which he had done, and he rested on the seventh day from all his work which he had done. Then God blessed the seventh day and sanctified it, because in it he rested from all his work which God had created and made. (Gen. 2:1-2 NKJV)

God could have ended the creation week on the sixth day after he made man. Then the days of the week would have been six and not seven. But he included the seventh to be a time of rest and refreshment and also contemplation of his created works. It is to be a time of meditation on the Creator and to reflect thoughtfully on all the things he has made, giving him praise and adoration. Thus the reason for observing the Sabbath reads:

Remember the Sabbath day, to keep it holy. Six days you shall labor and do all your work, but the seventh day is the Sabbath of the Lord your God. In it you shall do no work.... *For in six days the Lord made the heavens and the earth, the sea, and all that is in them, and rested the seventh day. Therefore, the Lord blessed the Sabbath day and hallowed it.* (Exod. 20:8-11 NKJV)

As the Lord did not work on the seventh day but rested, he asks us to do the same.

As much as the Sabbath is a sign of the creative work of God, it is also a sign of his redemptive work; because redemption is recreation and restoration to the original state. It is said of those who have been restored: "Therefore, if anyone is in Christ, he is a new creation; old things have passed away; behold, all things have become new" (2 Cor. 5:17 NKJV).

At the end of his redemptive work, as he hung on the cross, Jesus cried out, "It is finished." And when he cried thus, it was the eve of the Sabbath, and he entered into *death* and *rest*, and the Sabbath drew on. As the dead who *rest* from their *works*, Christ *rested* after he had *worked*.

The dead have ceased from their works, and those who are seeking perfection in character are not occupied with work. They are not people who spend all their time with work, neglecting to spend time alone with God. But, rather, they spend quality time with God through daily devotional Bible study, prayer, sharing the gospel and singing praises to God with hymns.

People whose time is occupied with work do not honor God. God had shown it to the prophet, Daniel, how men will be living in the time of the end. God says: "But you, Daniel, shut up the words, and seal the book until the time of the end; many shall run to and fro, and knowledge shall increase" (Dan. 12:4 NKJV).

As men are busy about life, seeking for themselves the riches and wealth of this life and not seeking to know God and to worship him, they will never find rest for their souls. But the plea of Jesus to men is, "Come to me, all you who labor and are heavy laden, and I will give you rest" (Matt. 11:28 NKJV).

It is only when we learn to die, that we can surrender all our toils and labor to Jesus; for then we would have ceased from all our works. Even the foolish of this world, the wicked, who will not surrender anything to God in this life, in death surrender all to God. When death lays its hands on the wicked, they leave their wealth, their hearts' desires, and their worldly pleasures behind; and they enter rest. Jesus tells the parable of a rich fool. He says:

> The ground of a certain rich man yielded plentifully. And
> he thought within himself, saying 'What shall I do, since

I have no room to store my crops?' So he said, I will do this: I will pull down my barns and build greater, and there I will store all my crops and my goods. And I will say to my soul, 'Soul, you have many goods laid up for many years; take your ease: eat, drink, and be merry.' But God said to him, 'You fool! This night your soul will be required of you; then whose will those things be which you have provided?' So is he who lays up treasure for himself, and is not rich toward God. (Luke 12:16-21 NKJV) Jesus again says: "For what shall it profit a man, if he shall gain the whole world, and lose his own soul? Or what shall a man give in exchange for his soul?" (Mark 8:36-37 KJV) Of such will be the end of many who will lose their souls. They, like the rich fool will in the end have gained the riches of the world at the cost of losing their souls.

God wants us to enter his rest and be as the dead who have nothing to worry about. In this life, we may have troubles and we may be afflicted with pain; but if we would enter God's rest, the Sabbath, we will die to our troubles and pain. Most important, God wants us to rest from the work of sin that we receive not of its wages.

If we should enter worship with God on the Sabbath day, the tempter and sin can have no dominion over us, and we enter the rest and perfect peace of God. Therefore, the word of God counsels us saying:

> Let us therefore fear, lest, a promise being left us of entering into his rest, any of you should seem to come short of it... For we which have believed do enter into rest, as he said, as I have sworn in my wrath, if they shall enter into my rest: although the works were finished from the foundation of the world. For he spake in a certain place of the seventh day on this wise, and God did rest the seventh day from all His *works*. And in this place again, if they shall enter into my rest. Seeing therefore it remaineth that some must enter therein,

and they to whom it was first preached entered not in because of unbelief: Again, he limiteth a certain day, saying in David, To day, after so long a time; as it is said, today if ye will hear His voice, harden not your hearts. For if Jesus had given them rest, then would he not afterward have spoken of another day. There remaineth therefore a rest to the people of God. For he that is entered into his rest, he also hath ceased from his own works, as God did from His. Let us labour therefore to enter into that rest, lest any man fall after the same example of unbelief. (Heb. 4:1-11 KJV).

If we should die to self, by having our mental disposition as the dead, and enter the worship of God every moment of the day with a song in our hearts, praising God with our lips, we will live all the days of our lives in a Sabbath rest. You have ceased from your works, and the problems and troubles in life have ceased to disturb you, for the dead have no worry of anything.

The way to enter into the joy and bliss of the Lord is death. When our lives ceases to be burdened with the troubles and toils of this life, we enter into the state of bliss. God's counsel to those who seek after his peace and the way to happiness is:

If thou turn away thy foot from the Sabbath, from doing thy pleasure on my holy day; and call the Sabbath a delight, the holy of the Lord, honourable; and shalt honour him, not doing thine own ways, nor finding thine own pleasure, nor speaking thine own words: Then shalt thou delight thyself in the Lord; and I will cause thee to ride upon the high places of the earth, and feed thee with the heritage of Jacob thy father: for the mouth of the Lord hath spoken it. (Isa. 58:13-14 KJV)

As God calls us into worship and asks us not to think our own thoughts or speak our own words or seek our own pleasure, he calls us into the sacrifice of self, that we may deny ourselves. For it is the dead who cannot think their own thoughts or speak their own words nor have their own pleasure. So, on the Sabbath day, God calls us to relinquish ownership of ourselves to him. If we desire to be happy, we must enter the Sabbath rest of God by having the mental disposition of the dead, and on the Sabbath day, observe God's sign to living a perfect life.

God has a sign. God's sign is a sign unto us that He is the Lord God, the Creator. The Scriptures say it plainly that God's sign is the Sabbath Law. God, speaking through the prophet, Ezekiel, says: "Hallow my Sabbaths, and they will be a sign between me and you, that you, may know that I am the Lord your God" (Ezek. 20:20 NKJV). Secondly, the sign of God is a sign unto us that, as God sanctified the Sabbath day and made it holy, so it is God who sanctifies us and makes us holy. God, still speaking through the prophet, Ezekiel, says: "Moreover I also gave them my Sabbaths, to be a sign between them and me that they might know that I am the Lord who sanctifies them" (Ezek. 20:12 NKJV). Thirdly, the Sabbath Law is the wink of God to all his children, for it is a sign to every believer, when Satan and sin shall be put to rest forever in the end of time at the last day. It is then that those who would have been made perfect by dying to self will be ushered into the kingdom of God to rest from the assault of Satan and sin.

The prophet, Nahum, speaking about the end of the reign of sin, says: "What do you conspire against the Lord? He will make an utter end of it. Affliction will not rise up a second time" (Nah. 1:9 NKJV).

The Sabbath, the seventh and the *last* day of the week, set aside by God as his holy day, reveals the unselfish character of God. God chooses to be last. As opposed to God's true day of worship, some have chosen the *first* day of the week to observe it. This reveals the selfish character of man; the "Me first" idea and the character of Satan; the one who seeks to be first all the time.

Through the ages, Satan, in an attempt to draw worship to himself and to deceive the nations, has substituted God's true day of worship with another day. Working through the church and the man of sin who sits in the temple showing himself that he is God, Satan has substituted God's day of worship with the first day instead of the last day. The prophet Daniel in prophecy, prophesied about a king who would seek to bring about this change. He wrote: "And he shall speak great words against the most High, and shall wear out the saints of the most High, and think to change *times* and *laws...*" (Dan. 7:25 KJV).

It was during the reign of the Roman Empire, and beginning with the Emperor Constantine, that God's true day of worship was supplanted by the first day of the week. It was the Emperor Constantine who first made a decree in A.D. 321 that Sunday, the first day of the week, be made a holy day. This was later adopted by the Roman Catholic Church who, claiming to have authority to change or modify the laws of God, in the council of Laodicea in A.D. 336, transferred the solemnity from Saturday to Sunday. The Protestant reformers in the age of the reformation failed to revert the Sabbath to its original day, some giving the reason for the change that, because Jesus rose on the first day of the week, Sunday has become the day of the Lord and the new Sabbath. But God's day of worship, which has embedded in it his principle of perfection and completion, has always been and will always be Saturday, the seventh and last day of the week.

Those who live as though they are dead have died to sin. They follow the counsel of God, which comes through Paul, saying: "Likewise you also, reckon yourselves to be dead indeed to sin, but alive to God in Christ Jesus our Lord." (Rom. 6:11 NKJV). Moreover, they die daily as the apostle, Paul, who said, "I affirm, by the boasting in you which I have in Christ Jesus our Lord, I die daily" (1 Cor. 15:31 NKJV). And to die daily is to enter into the Sabbath rest of God. You have ceased from the works of sin, and you live your life in worship and in service to God. But those people who do not obey God in his command, "have no rest day or night, who worship the beast and his image, and whoever receives the mark of his name." (Rev. 14:11

NKJV). They have no rest because they do not choose to enter into the Sabbath rest of God.

Holiness is wrought in death. The dead do not sin. And in death, there is the perfect keeping of the commandments of God. If we would be as the dead and cease from the works of sin, the only law we would need to know is the Fourth Commandment, the Sabbath law that we may be kept in remembrance of having entered into the rest and peace of God. For, since they have died and ceased from these acts, where is the need to tell the dead, thou shalt not kill or thou shalt not steal or thou shalt not commit adultery or thou shalt not covet? To this end, the apostle Paul says: "But the fruit of the Spirit is love, joy, peace, long-suffering, gentleness, goodness, faith, meekness, temperance: *against such, there is no law.* And they that are Christ's have *crucified* the flesh with the affections and lusts" (Gal. 5:22-24 KJV)

The reason why the law of God has been written, and with negatives, is that men live to commit these acts of sin. Because men live to commit these sins, God tells us not to do them. And the way to cease from committing these sins is to be as the dead. For the reason the Fourth Commandment will keep us in remembrance of having entered into death and rest, God begins the Fourth Commandment by saying: "Remember the Sabbath day, to keep it holy," as holiness is wrought in death.

It is by the grace and mercy of God, he lets men die, so they may be freed from sin and the forces of evil. In death, the righteous are removed from the earth and hidden from the power of the tempter forever. Thus, the prophet, Isaiah, says: "The righteous perishes, and no man takes it to heart; merciful men are taken away, while no one considers that the righteous is taken away from evil" (Isa. 57:1 NKJV).

To every man who is seeking the salvation of God comes the counsel of God through the prophet, Isaiah, saying:

> Thus says the Lord: "Keep justice, and do righteousness
> for my salvation is about to come, and my righteousness
> to be revealed. Blessed is the man who does this, and

the son of man who lays hold, on it; who keeps from defiling the Sabbath, and keeps his hand from doing any evil." (Isa. 56:1-2 NKJV)

Through eternal ages, the redeemed of the earth will observe the Sabbath. God speaks through the prophet, Isaiah, saying:

For as the new heavens and the new earth which I will make shall remain before me, says the Lord, so shall your descendants and your name remain. And it shall come to pass that from one new moon to another, and from one Sabbath to another, all flesh shall come to worship before me, says the LORD (Isa. 66:22-23 NKJV)

# THE PRINCIPLE OF THE PERFECT LIFE

The fourth commandment is a law and a principle to be obeyed and observed. As a law, it is to be obeyed and observed among the children of God, every seventh and last day of the week. As a principle, it is to be observed every day as the guiding principle, in all aspects of our lives. This perpetual commandment is to be observed as God's sign to sanctification and holiness and for that reason his way to living the perfect life. God speaks through the prophet Ezekiel saying: "Moreover also I gave them my Sabbaths, to be a sign between me and them, that they might know that I am the Lord that sanctify them" (Ezek.20:12KJV). The Sabbath and all that it entails is the secret to living a perfect life.

As a principle, the children of God are to live every day of their lives as the last day of a man's life on earth; the day of one's death. As the dead, they are not to seek first place in anything but the last. For as the dead who have no portion in the things of the earth, the one who lives as though he is dead is as one who does not have any portion in the things of the earth.

In every aspect of our lives, we must not seek the first place or the first portion, but the last. The one who seeks to be the last in everything, observes the principle in the fourth commandment, which is the seventh day as last among the days of the week and which does not share in the creation works of God and neither is it to have a share in the works of man as commanded by God. In his creation of the heavens and the earth, God did not do any work on the seventh and last day, and in like manner he commands man not to work on the last day. Being last, is the great principle in the seventh day as the last day of the week.

The life of the person who is last in everything is not fraught with covetousness, neither ambition nor anxiety, and he does not compete with any one for supremacy. Rather, as the dead whose work has come to an end, and who are content with their estate, the one who seeks to be the last in everything is content with whatever his estate might be, and his soul is filled with the peace of God. As the dead who are humbled in the grave, he lives in the spirit of humility and sees all others as better than himself.

> In his discourse with the young rich ruler, Jesus said to him: "If you want to be perfect, go, sell what you have and give to the poor, and you will have treasure in heaven; and come, and follow me." (Matt.19:21 NKJV). When the young man went away sorrowful because he had great possessions, Jesus then turned to his disciples and said to them: "Assuredly, I say to you that it is hard for a rich man to enter the kingdom of heaven. And again I say to you, it is easier for a camel to go through the eye of a needle than for a rich man to enter the kingdom of God." (Matt 19:23-24 NKJV). The disciples astonished at that saying of Jesus, also asked him, saying: "Who then can be saved?" (Matt 19:25 NKJV). Jesus next said to them: "With men this is impossible, but with God all things are possible." (Matt. 19:26 NKJV). Then Peter said to him; "See, we have left all and followed you. Therefore what shall we have?" (Matt. 19:27 NKJV). So, Jesus said to them:

> Assuredly I say to you, that in the regeneration, when the Son of Man sits on the throne of his glory, you who have followed me will also sit on twelve thrones, judging the twelve tribes of Israel. And everyone who has left houses or brothers or sisters or father or mother or wife or children or lands, for my name's sake, shall

receive a hundredfold, and inherit eternal life. But many who are first will be last, and the last first. (Matt. 19:28-30 NKJV).

The saying of Jesus, "Many who are first will be last, and the last first," though in very simple words, are coded, which requires decoding with explanation. The codes in the statement are the words, *first* and *last*. What do these coded words represent and what are the decoding words?

*Life* is synonymous with the *first day*. The very day a man is born into the earth, to be among the living, is the *first day* of that man being *alive*. In contrast, *death* is synonymous with the *last day*. The day on which a man *dies* is the *last day* of the man's life. This meaning, on our *first day* we *live*, and on our *last day* we die. Therefore, *first* represent the *living* and *last* represent the *dead*. The decoding words therefore are *life* and *death*. *First* is the code representing the *living* and *last* represents the *dead*.

As realized that *first* represent the *living* and *last* represent the *dead*, the coded statement of Jesus: "Many who are *first* will be *last*, and the *last first*", will translate to read: "Many who are *living* shall *die*, and the *dead* shall *live*." What then is the intended meaning of this saying of Jesus?

In the story of the rich young ruler who was seeking what he must do to inherit eternal life, he was not ready to do what it takes to obtain eternal life. He would not be as the *dead* whose wealth and riches and all that they own are given to others. At the saying of Jesus, "go, sell what you have and give to the poor, and you will have treasure in heaven," he went away sorrowful. He would rather be *alive* and not as the *dead*, to learn the lessons of *self-denial*.

In the end of time, at the appearing of Christ, at the *last day*, all those who had sought to *preserve their lives*, to *live* as they please, *and would not surrender their lives to God, will die*. But those *who surrender their lives to God, to live as the dead who have died, and in dying have died to sin, shall live*. This is what Jesus meant when he said, "For whoever desires to *save* his *life* will *lose* it, but whoever *loses his life* for my sake will find it. For what profit is it to a man if he gains the whole world, and loses his own soul? Or what will a man give in exchange for his soul?" (Matt. 16:25-26, NKJV)

The saying of Jesus: "Many who are *first* will be *last*, and the *last first*," has many cross-references in the scriptures, saying the same thing in other words and using different illustrations. The following are some of those cross-references: "If anyone desires to come after me, let him *deny* himself, and take up his *cross*, and follow me. For whoever desires to *save* his life will *lose* it, but whoever *loses* his life for my sake will find it." (Matt.16:24-25, NKJV). "And whoever *exalts* himself will be *humbled*, and he who *humbles* himself will be *exalted*." (Matt. 23:12 NKJV). Also using the illustration of a grain of wheat, Jesus says: "Most assuredly, I say to you, unless a grain of wheat falls into the ground and *dies*, it remains alone; but if it *dies*, it produces much grain. He who loves his *life* will *lose* it, and he who *hates* his *life* in this world will keep it for eternal life." (John 12:24-25 NKJV).

Those who seek to *save* their *lives* are those who seek to *preserve* their *lives* to enjoy the pleasures of sin. If they were given eternity to *live*, they would *live* as they please and not as God would want them to *live*. Those who *love their lives of sin* and *live* to enjoy the pleasures of sin *will lose their lives* and the pleasures they enjoy at the *last day*. In the *end*, they will *die* and *cease* from their *works of sin* and enter *rest*. "Many who are *first* will be *last*." In the grave, by their irresponsiveness to sin and everything else, the great principle in the fourth commandment, the Sabbath law – to be the *last* and not *first*, and to *rest* from your *works*, will be accomplished in them.

Who are *last day* people? They are people who have *ceased from sinning* because they are like the *dead who do not sin*. There are two groups of *last day* people. *The first group of last day people*, are, *those who choose to be last day people*. They are those who though *alive*, have *died to sin* and have been set free from the bondage of sin, by the power of God. They *have put to death* the *works* of the flesh and *live lives of self-denial*. This is the essence of baptism. The apostle Paul expounding on the doctrine of baptism says:

Or do you not know that as many of us as were *baptized* into Christ Jesus were *baptized* into his *death*? Therefore we were *buried* with him through *baptism* into *death*, that just as Christ was raised from the *dead* by the glory of the father, even so we also should walk in newness of life. For if we have been united together in the likeness of his *death*, certainly we also shall be in the likeness of his resurrection, knowing this, that our old man was *crucified* with him, that the body of sin might be done away with, that we should no longer be slaves of sin. For he who has *died* has been freed from sin. Now if we *died* with Christ, we believe that we shall also *live* with him." (Rom. 6:3-8, NKJV).

In the end, those who have learned to be last, will be first. That is, those who have learned to die, will live.

Those who choose to be *last day people, cease* from their *works* on the *seventh* and last *day* of every week to keep *the Sabbath* holy. They *observe the Sabbath day* as a law and a principle, and a sign unto that *last day* when God shall *end the work of sin*. In that *last day*, God's *holiness*, which is wrought in *the principle of the last day*, shall prevail eternally. To this end the prophet Isaiah prophesies, saying: "Thus says the Lord: 'Keep justice, and do righteousness for my salvation is about to come, and my righteousness to be revealed. Blessed is the man who does this, and the son of man who lays hold on it; who keeps from defiling *the Sabbath*, and keeps his hand from doing any evil." (Isa. 56: 1-2 NKJV).

The second group of last day people, are, *those who would not choose to be last day people*, but will *wait* to be made last day people, at the appearing of Christ, at the last day. As Jesus mingled with the children of Israel, he said to them: "Verily I say unto you, that there be some of them that stand here, *which shall not taste of death*, till they have seen the kingdom of God come with power." Mark (9:1 KJV) Jesus had earlier said to them: "Whosoever will come after me, let him *deny himself and take up his cross*, and follow me. For whosoever will save his life shall lose it; but whosoever shall lose his life for my sake and the gospel's the same shall save it. For what shall it profit a man, if he shall gain the whole world, and lose his own soul? Or what shall a man give in exchange for his soul? (Mark 8:34 – 37 KJV)

In the end, one way or the other, everybody will be of the last day people, the seventh-day people. Either we choose to be last day people as we live, or we wait to be made last day people, at the last day, on the day of the Lord's appearing. Those who choose to be last day people will live, but those who wait to be made last day people will die. Those who choose to be last day people have died to sin but those who wait to be made last day people are alive unto sin. Therefore, the apostle Paul says: "For if you live according to the flesh you will die; but if by the Spirit you put to death the deeds of the body, you will live." (Rom. 8:13 NKJV)

Life and death are real, and all intelligent beings have experienced life, but not everyone has experienced death and what it means to die. Except the Creator who has created both life and death explain to us what it means to die, death will always remain a mystery to the living.

The great principle of the last day is death to sin. The Lord and Judge of that day is himself the principle of that day. No sin can abide in the presence of God and in the day when he shall reveal himself unto all men, sin and sinners will be destroyed. His death on the cross was to demonstrate the nature of his character, and for all intelligent beings and all who seek after his wisdom to visualize the principle by which he lives.

The day of death, the last day on earth for every man, ends the work of man, and he enters rest. If he lived a life of sin, he ceases from his work of sin and to sin no more. In like manner, the last day of earth's history, will end the work of every man, and all shall enter rest. In that day, everybody will abide by the great principle of the last day one way or the other. None shall escape the keeping of the great principle of the last day. Those who lived abiding by the principle of the last day, to them shall be given life eternal. But those who lived never to abide by the principle of the last day shall die to abide by that principle.

The day is coming when the originator of sin and all the workers of evil shall abide by the principle of the last day. In that day they shall rest from all their works, and they shall have their good night sleep in eternal hell. In the meantime, Satan and his host of wicked angels are waiting to be last. The Lord God Almighty will come in the last day, and with the blast of fire and brimstone, Satan and his angels will become the last. Thus, Jude in his epistle, says: "And the angels which kept not their first estate, but left their own habitation, he hath reserved in everlasting chains under darkness unto the judgment of the great day." (Jude 6 KJV)

Death, though the consequence of sin, is to the contrary God's principle to life. That is, if you sin you will die, but if you die to sin, you will live. Those who find this principle and allow themselves to be empowered by the Spirit of God to abide by it, have found the way to eternal life. To those who live by the principle of the last day, if they have died, they shall resurrect, and in their resurrection, they shall be as those who have been baptized. This is the essence and purpose of baptism. Having died to sin in life, and buried in the earth, the dead in Christ shall rise and live unto righteousness forevermore. They are the seeds of God sown in the ground, awaiting the harvest of the earth, at the last day. In death and buried in the earth, they are like seeds sown in the ground, which first dies and later sprouts from the ground. The apostle John in vision seeing the harvest of the earth says:

> And I heard a voice from heaven saying unto me, write, blessed are the dead which die in the Lord from henceforth: Yea, saith the Spirit, that they may rest from their labours; and their works do follow them. And I looked, and behold a white cloud, and upon the cloud one sat like unto the Son of man, having on his head a golden crown, and in his hand a sharp sickle. And another angel came out of the temple, crying with a loud voice to him that sat on the cloud, thrust in thy sickle, and reap; for the harvest of the earth is ripe. And he that sat on the cloud thrust in his sickle on the earth; and the earth was reaped. (Rev. 14:13-16 KJV)

After Adam and Eve sinned, God in passing judgment upon them said to the woman: "I will greatly multiply thy sorrow and thy conception; in sorrow thou shalt bring forth children." (Gen. 3:16 KJV). This judgment upon the woman was not an arbitrary judgment, but a pronouncement foretelling the effect of sin on the woman and her children.

God made the earth to be inhabited with people. At the dawn of creation, God said to the man and the woman, "Be fruitful, and multiply, and replenish the earth, and subdue it." (Gen 1:28 KJV) But during the reign of sin, the work of evil on the earth has robbed her of many of her children. The earth, which is the mother of the children of the earth, is like a pregnant woman suffering from labor pains, waiting to deliver her child. The "Labor pains" the earth is enduring is the work of evil being worked on it. As evil doers traverse the earth, the earth suffers birth pangs, waiting to deliver her children.

All those who chose to be last day people, and have since died, and are buried in the earth, are like children in the womb of their expectant mother, waiting to be delivered. On the last day, the Deliverer will come and deliver Mother Earth from her labor pains, by putting an end to the work of sin. Mother Earth shall give birth to her children, and she shall have a Sabbath rest from her labor pains. In that day, the true children of the earth shall be made manifest, and there shall be no more pain of the labor of sin. The work of sin, which has so much robbed the earth of many of her children, is ended, and the breath of holiness pulsates through her redeemed children.

Looking to that day when the sufferings of Mother Earth and her children shall come to an end, the apostle Paul wrote: *"For I reckon that the sufferings of this present time are not worthy to be compared with the glory which shall be revealed in us. For the earnest expectation of the creature waiteth for the manifestation of the sons of God. For the creature was made subject to vanity, not willingly, but by reason of him who hath subjected the same in hope, because the creature itself also shall be delivered from the bondage of corruption into the glorious liberty of the children of God. For we know that the whole creation groaneth and travaileth in pain together until now. And not only they, but ourselves also, which have the first fruits of the Spirit, even we ourselves groan within ourselves, waiting for the adoption, to wit, the redemption of our body." (Romans 8:18 – 23 KJV)*

The scriptures tell us that the day before the Sabbath day, is the day of preparation towards the Sabbath day. The events surrounding the death of Jesus make it known that the sixth day is the preparation day towards the Sabbath day. Luke recording events that followed the death of Jesus says: *"And, behold, there was a man named Joseph, a counselor; and he was a good man, and a just: (The same had not consented to the counsel and deed of them;) he was of Arimathea, a city of the Jews: who also himself waited for the kingdom of God. This man went unto Pilate, and begged the body of Jesus. And he took it down, and wrapped it in linen, and laid it in a sepulchre that was hewn in stone, wherein never man before was laid. And that day was the preparation, and the Sabbath drew on. And the women also, which came with him from Galilee, followed after, and beheld the sepulchre, and how his body was laid. And they returned, and prepared spices and ointments; and rested the Sabbath day according to the commandment." (Luke 23:50 – 56 KJV)*

As Friday, the sixth day is the day of preparation towards the Sabbath day, in like manner, this present time, is as the day of preparation towards the last day of the struggle between good and evil. This probationary time is the preparation time towards the day when every man's work shall come to an end. It is the preparation to that day when everybody, both men and angels shall become last day people.

The Sabbath day is called "the Lord's day." The apostle John who received visions about the end times on the Isle of Patmos, in giving his testimony to those things he saw, says: "I was in the Spirit on the Lord's day, and heard behind me a great voice, as of a trumpet." (Rev. 1:10 KJV) John was referring to that day over which the Son of man is Lord. The Lord declares about himself, saying: "For the Son of man is Lord even of the Sabbath day." (Matt 12:8 KJV) The prophets also make mention of "the day of the Lord." It is the day in which the Lord will visit his vengeance on sin and the wicked. This will be the last day of the work of sin on earth, and the Lord will bring to completion his work of salvation. He will then shout from his throne and say: "it is done." (Rev. 16:17 KJV) The prophet Zephaniah prophesies about " the day of the Lord," saying: "The great day of the

Lord is near, it is near, and hasteth greatly, even the voice of the day of the Lord: the mighty man shall cry there bitterly. That day is a day of wrath, a day of trouble and distress, a day of wasteness and desolation, a day of darkness and gloominess, a day of clouds and thick darkness." (Zeph. 1:14 – 15 KJV)

There are similarities in "the Lord's day" and "the day of the Lord." "The Lord's day" is the seventh and last day of the week, in which the Lord tells us to keep the day holy and not to do any work. "The day of the Lord," which is the day of his appearing, will also be the last day of the work of sin on earth, and the day when every man's work shall come to an end. It is also the day when God's holiness shall prevail eternally. This gives indication that the day of the Lord, the day on which the Lord shall appear to end the work of sin, will be the seventh and last day of the week, which is the Lord's day.

In the end, "the day of the Lord," the day of his appearing, will be on "the Lord's day." The end of God's salvation work will coincide with the *end* of the work of every man. In that day every man will be like the dead who do not do any work. The earth and all its inhabitants will enter into a Sabbath rest on the day of the Lord, the last day of the history of humanity. "The first," those who lived according to the desires of the flesh, will be slain by the brightness of the Lord's appearing and by the breath of his mouth, to become "the last." Then "the last," those who died to sin, will resurrect to life to become, "the first."

The whole controversy between good and evil is about choosing to be first or last, and what it means to be first or last. Satan chooses to be first, but God chooses to be last. In the end, God shall reveal himself at the last day to be proved of all men. At the appearing of the Father, all those who lived trusting in His word and died to sin, will be exalted to be His children. But those who never lived by the principle of dying to sin will be humbled. It is only when we die that we become like God. "The first shall be last and the last first." Those who choose to live will die but those who choose to die will live.

At the appearing of Jesus, all those who chose to be last day people will be manifested on the last day, the seventh day, as the dwelling place and sanctuary of God. The Spirit of God will be housed in them forever. Then shall be brought to pass the saying: "Behold, the tabernacle of God is with men, and he will dwell with them, and they shall be his people, and God himself shall be with them, and be their God." (Rev. 21:3 KJV) That last day will be the fulfillment of the prophecy of Jesus about the temple of God, which says: "Him that overcometh will I make a pillar in the temple of my God…." (Rev. 3:12 KJV)

Those who would become the sanctuary of God are the people who have become perfect in character like God by obeying and keeping the principle of the last day which is the principle of the seventh day. These are those who would have washed their garments in the blood of the Lamb of God to be completely cleansed from sin, and to appear in character and nature like God.

In that last day when all the redeemed of the earth shall appear in character and nature looking like God, then shall be fulfilled the scripture which says, "Behold what manner of love the Father hath bestowed upon us, that we should be called the sons of God: therefore the world knoweth us not, because it knew him not. Beloved, now are we the sons of God, and it doth not yet appear what we shall be: but we know that, when he shall appear, we shall be like him; for we shall see him as he is." (1 John 3:1-2 KJV)

The death of Jesus was the demonstration of the nature and character of God. God lives as one who is dead. The mystery of death therefore is the greatest discovery to be made by every intelligent being. To make this discovery and to live by it is to be like God in nature and character. In heaven, Lucifer had desired to be like the Most High God. That way which he has been searching for to be like the Most High God is found in death which is the principle of the last day. So, the day is coming, and it will be the last day for Satan to go the way by which one can be like God. In the pit of hell, Lucifer will become like the Most High God. At last, in the end, on the last day, he would have found the way.

The day is coming when everybody will become like God one way or the other. Those who choose to live by the principle of the last day will rise in the last day and be exalted to be like God. But those who never lived by the principle of the last day will be humbled in death, and there to be like God.

92

# THE NUMBER SEVEN AND PERFECTION

The number *seven* denotes *last*. The *seventh day* is the *last day* of the week. In the creation of the heavens and the earth, God created the days of the week and he made the seventh day to be the last day. As the last day of the week, the seventh day is the day that seals up the weekly cycle bringing the cycle to completion.

As noted, the number seven also denotes completion and perfection. In his purposes God uses the number seven to denote completion and perfection. There are the seven churches, the seven stars, the seven candlesticks, the seven seals, the seven trumpets, the seven thunders, the seven plagues and the seven golden vials of the wrath of God, all in the book of Revelation, and the seventh of every one of them brings to completion a purpose of God.

In the days of Joseph in the land of Egypt, there were the seven years of plenty, and the seven years of famine and the seventh year of both times brought to completion the purposes of God. Also, in the days of Elijah after the three and a half years of drought in Israel and after God had sent fire to manifest his glory before the people, it took Elijah praying seven times before there came rain.

King Nebuchadnezzar came back to his senses and humbled himself before God in the seventh year after he became like a beast and lived in the field with beasts. In the seventh year when his understanding returned to him, Nebuchadnezzar gave praise to God and testified to the greatness of God, saying: "And at the end of the days I Nebuchadnezzar lifted up my eyes unto heaven, and my understanding returned unto me, and I blessed the most High, and I praised and honoured him that liveth forever, whose dominion is an everlasting dominion, and his kingdom is from generation to generation: And all the inhabitants of the earth are reputed as nothing: and he doeth according to his will in the army of heaven, and among the inhabitants of the earth: and none can stay his hand, or say unto him, what doest thou?"(Daniel 4:34-35 KJV)

God also created the heavens and the earth and the things in them in six days and rested the seventh day bringing his work of creation to completion. And at the completion of his creative work, God did something special for the seventh day which he did not do for any of the other six days. The creation account on what God did for the seventh day says:

> Thus, the heavens and the earth were finished (completed), and all the host of them. And on the seventh day God ended (completed) his work which he had made; and he rested on the seventh day from all his work which he had made. And God *blessed* the seventh day and *sanctified* it: because that in it he had rested from all his work which God created and made. (Gen. 2:1-2 KJV).

> As stated in the scripture, God *blessed* the seventh day and *sanctified* it; which means he set it apart from the other six days, because in it he did no work but rested.

Also, as the last day of God's created works, the seventh day is the seal of God's creation. In the first six days of creation God worked but on the seventh day he did not work but rested. The seventh day, therefore, was made specifically for rest. It is the day void of work. The seventh day is the Sabbath day and Sabbath means rest.

The seventh day is set aside by God as a day of rest; that man may rest from his works as God did from his work of creation. In the Fourth Commandment of the Ten Commandments for all men and for all time, God says expressly: "Remember the Sabbath day, to keep it holy. Six days shalt thou labor, and do all thy work: But the seventh day is the

Sabbath of the Lord thy God: in it thou shalt not do any work, thou, nor thy son, nor thy daughter, thy manservant, nor thy maidservant, nor thy cattle, nor thy stranger that is within thy gates: For in six days the Lord made heaven and earth, the sea, and all that in them is, and *rested* the seventh day: wherefore the Lord blessed the Sabbath day and *hallowed* it. (Exod. 20:8-11 KJV)

The number seven also represents a rest time for the earth. The earth regains its topsoil through the decay (death) and decomposition of leaves and other living organisms. God had instructed the children of Israel as he spoke to Moses in Mount Sinai, saying:

> Speak unto the children of Israel, and say unto them, when ye come into the land which I give you, then shall the land keep a Sabbath unto the Lord. Six years thou shalt sow thy field, and six years thou shalt prune thy vineyard, and gather in the fruit thereof; but in the seventh year shall be a Sabbath of rest unto the land, a Sabbath for the Lord: thou shalt neither sow thy field, nor prune thy vineyard. That which groweth of its own accord of thy harvest thou shalt not reap, neither gather the grapes of thy vine undressed: for it is a year of rest unto the land. And the Sabbath of the land shall be meat for you; for thee, and for thy servant, and for thy maid, and for thy hired servant, and for thy stranger that sojourneth with thee. And for thy cattle, and for the beast that are in thy land, shall all the increase thereof be meat. (Lev. 25:1-7 KJV)

The seventh day as the last day of the week and the day of rest, also symbolize the last day on earth for every man, when man takes rest from his works. When men die, they enter their last day. The day on which every man dies becomes their last day on earth. Therefore, the last day on earth for every man becomes the place where the dead go to rest. That is to say, the dwelling place of the dead, is in the last day. The last day, therefore, is synonymous with death.

God lives by the principle of the dead. Since God lives as one who is dead, his sanctuary and dwelling place is in the last day, the seventh day, which symbolizes the place of the dead and which is also the dwelling place of those who have died to sin.

The righteousness of God is wrought in death and in dying to sin. The dead do not steal, they do not kill, they do not commit adultery, they do not worship idols, they do not bear false witness, they do not covet anything, and being dead they have entered their last day and they are resting from their works. This gives the reason why the place of the sanctuary of God is the seventh and last day of the week. Therefore, those who come into the sanctuary of God to worship him and to be like him in holiness and righteousness, have made the place of the dead, the seventh and last day, their sanctuary. And in this place, they have ceased from sinning. In all the days of their lives, they live in a Sabbath rest, set free from the bondage of sin and made perfect in holiness. Like the Rock of Ages, the chief cornerstone of the church and sanctuary, their minds have become impregnable to sin and they are the lively stones building up the heavenly sanctuary of God which transcends the earth going up into heaven.

When men die, they bring all their work to an end and they enter rest. The last day on earth for every man is therefore the time of rest for man. We rightfully erect tombstones over the dead with the inscription, "Rest in peace." In like manner, the seventh and last day of the week, the Sabbath day of the Lord and Sabbath which means rest, is the resting place of God and all those who come into his sanctuary. Therefore, God bids all who come into his dwelling place, the place of the dead, to rest from their work on the Sabbath day. The reason being that, in the place of the dead there is no work.

The seventh and last day of the week, the day which denotes completion and perfection is the place where God has established his sanctuary and church. It is in this day that is to be found the principle of death to sin which is the principle of holiness and perfection. As the last day of the week and the day set aside for rest, it symbolizes the day of rest on earth for every man; the day of death when man takes rest from his works. Thus, the principles of the seventh day are, last, death and rest. These principles of the seventh day and the fourth commandment, are what amounts to the science of the cross. They are also the principles of the love and peace of God. Therefore, the apostle John says about the love of God which the children of God are to emulate, saying: "Hereby perceive we the love of God, because he laid down his life for us: and we ought to lay down our lives for the brethren." (1 John 3:16 KJV)

The principle of laying down our lives for our brethren is to be found in the principles of last and death in the seventh day. As Jesus taught his disciples, he spoke to them about his impended death and said to them, saying: "Greater love has no one than this, than to lay down one's life for his friends." (John 15:13 NKJV) So, Jesus, at the end of his sojourn on earth, died for the sins of the world. In like manner, when at last Satan shall be brought into the last day to die, he will lay down his life for all mankind and the earth. So, if Lucifer wants to be friends with the children of this world, in the day that he shall die, he would then have learned to do as Jesus says, "Greater love has no one than this, than to lay down one's life for his friends." (John 15:13 NKJV) In that day, when at last Satan shall perish in the fires of hell, his life will be as a sacrifice for the earth and the earth will be rid of sin and its perpetrators. The earth, which has been the place of the work of sin will at last have her rest.

Therefore, by the unchangeable principles of the seventh and last day, all those who come to the place of the sanctuary of God, come to the place of death to sin, and they shall find peace and rest unto their souls. The seventh day is therefore a perpetual day of holy convocation. God had said to the children of Israel: "Six days shall work be done: but the seventh day is the Sabbath of rest, a holy convocation; ye shall do no work therein: it is the Sabbath of the Lord in all your dwellings." (Lev. 23:3 KJV)

When the Holy One of Israel dwelt among men, it was said of him: "And he came to Nazareth, where he had been brought up: and, as his custom was, he went into the synagogue on the Sabbath day, and stood up for to read." (Luke 4:16 KJV) It was the custom of Jesus when he dwelt here on earth to worship God on the Sabbath day.

God also declares the Sabbath to be a holy convocation throughout eternal ages, saying, "For as the new heavens and the new earth, which

I will make, shall remain before me, saith the Lord, so shall your seed and your name remain. And it shall come to pass, that from one new moon to another, and from one Sabbath to another, shall all flesh come to worship before me, saith the Lord." (Isa. 66:22-23, KJV)

The principles of last, death and rest in the seventh day, the sanctuary and dwelling place of God, are the powers and weapons by which God will destroy Satan and all the wicked. On the day of the Lord, when he shall return to the earth, that day will be the last day cut off for the work of sin. Lucifer, the originator of sin, has not learned to be last and to live by the principle of being last. Instead, Lucifer incites the children of the earth to seek to be first in all areas of their lives. So, in the day of the Lord, God will bring Lucifer and all who live by the principle of being first into the last day, that there, they may be last. "The first shall be last and the last first."

The day is coming, and it will be the Lord's day, the Sabbath and seventh day, when this angel who seeks to usurp the authority of God and to be crowned as "Lucifer the First," will become "Lucifer the Last." In that day, Lucifer's pride and his contention with the laws of God, which has resulted in the manifestation and display of sin in all forms, will come to an end.

The seventh day, therefore, is the place where Satan, sin and all sinners will be crushed with the thunderous power of God to usher in eternal holiness and righteousness. This place is the place of death to sin. So, says the commandment, "Remember the Sabbath day to keep it holy." And in this place, all who have been trampling on God's holiness and righteousness will perish. It is in this place that they will find their final resting place and to sin no more. God will bring Satan into the last day that there he will see his last and become the last.

Although Satan will burn a long time in hellfire and suffer for all the wickedness he has caused in God's creation, he will eventually be consumed in the fire and burn to ashes. For this is the prophecy which God gave to the prophet Malachi when he said:

For, behold, the day cometh, that shall burn as an oven; and all the proud, yea, and all that do wickedly, shall be stubble: and the day that cometh shall burn them up, saith the Lord of hosts, that it shall leave them neither root nor branch. But unto you that fear my name shall the Sun of Righteousness arise with healing in his wings; and ye shall go forth, and grow up as calves of the stall. And ye shall tread down the wicked: for they shall be ashes under the soles of your feet in the day that I shall do this, saith the Lord of hosts (Mal. 4:1-3 KJV)

Therefore, in the end of the controversy between God and Satan, when Satan shall finally perish in hellfire, he will die and cease from sinning. In that day, he will enter his last day and forever make the last day his dwelling place and there to find his eternal rest and never to rise again. At last, "Lucifer the First" will become "Lucifer the Last." "The first shall be last."

It has been the desire of Satan that men will live in sin and in disobedience to God and never die. In his temptation to Eve, Satan said to her, "You shall not surely die". But what Lucifer, this king of fools who exalts his word above the word of God, should know about his own deeds and to understand to get the wisdom of God, is that, as he has become a murderer destroying men, he brings them into their last day, that there, they may die and sin no more. Through sin which has resulted in death, Satan brings the work of men to an end and they enter rest. In death, the perpetrators of sin cease from sinning.

The principles of the seventh and last day which the unrighteous have been disobeying, will at last be fulfilled in them on the last day on earth. On that day of the Lord, the powers of the principles of the last day, which are last, death and rest, will be fulfilled in everybody. Sin and sinners will see their last time and become the last. In that last day, they shall receive the just recompense of sin, which is death. The unrighteous shall then cease to exist and forever rest from their works. But those who have chosen to live by the principles of the last day, by dying to sin, will resurrect to life, and forever live by the principles of the last day.

It therefore behooves everybody who wants to be like God, to come to the place of last, and there die to sin. This place is the seventh day where God's sanctuary is erected. Those who have willingly come to the place of last, have through baptism died to sin. They are those who have washed their garments in the blood of the Lamb of God, to be completely cleansed from sin and to appear in character and in nature like God. And it is in the sanctuary of God, that they are being transformed into the image of God by the principles of the sanctuary. They are like Naaman, who washed in the Jordan River, and after the seventh wash, became completely healed of the disease of leprosy. Naaman was completely healed of leprosy after the seventh wash because after the seventh wash he reached God's number for completion and perfection.

It has been Lucifer's desire to be like the most High God; He who is "the First and the Last" (Rev. 1:11). Lucifer the First, who seeks to be first all the time, must also come to the place of last and there die to become Lucifer the Last. The Lord Jesus Christ, the most High God, the One who is "the First and the Last" (Rev. 1:11) came to the earth and died. So, since it has been Lucifer's desire to be like the Most High, which is Jesus and who is the "First and the Last," Lucifer must come to the place of last to be like Jesus who on His last day on earth, died. It is only then that Lucifer's desire to be like the most High God, will be completed and perfected, and it will only be at the place of completion and perfection, which is the seventh day. In that day of the Lord, Satan's work will be ended, and it will be like when God finished his work of creation and ended it on the seventh day, the day God blessed and hallowed. In that day, as Satan perishes in the fires of hell, he will cease from sinning and become like God who is sinless. God will cast Satan into hellfire to let Satan prove that he can endure the fire like God who is a consuming fire and dwells in light unapproachable.

In the end, at the last day, shall be fulfilled the principle, "The first shall be last and the last first." Whosoever chooses to be first shall be last and whosoever chooses to be last shall be first. That is, those who never want to die to sin shall die and those who have chosen to die to sin shall live. Those who choose to be first are those who live unto self and never want to die, but those who choose to be last are those who live lives of self-denial and have put to death sin in their lives.

The time of the rest of God, is to be found in the seventh day the last day of the week, the day that God has set aside for rest. For we rest only after we have worked and that is in the last day of work. In modern times, we hear people say they are taking a sabbatical, and it is after they have worked hard.

The writer of the book of Hebrews refers to the seventh day as the perpetual resting place of God and sounds a warning to all believers who may choose another day thinking that Jesus has given us another day of rest. The apostle Paul, who is believed to have written the epistle to the Hebrews, says:

> For we which have believed do enter into rest, as he said, As I have sworn in my wrath, if they shall enter into my rest: although the works were finished from the foundation of the world. For he spake in a certain place of the seventh day on this wise, And God did rest the seventh day from all his works. And in this place again, if they shall enter into my rest. Seeing therefore it remaineth that some must enter therein, and they to whom it was first preached entered not in because of unbelief: Again, he limiteth a certain day, saying in David, Today, after so long a time; as it is said, Today if ye will hear his voice, harden not your hearts. For if Jesus had given them rest, then would he not afterward have spoken of another day. There remaineth therefore a rest to the people of God. For he that is entered into his rest, he also hath ceased from his own works, as God did from his. Let us labor therefore to enter into that rest, lest any man fall after the same example of unbelief" (Heb. 4:3-11 KJV).

> That rest we are to labor and to enter in is the Sabbath rest of the seventh day which is embodied in the Fourth Commandment of the Ten Commandments, the moral and perpetual laws of God.

Death is the principle by which we live to become perfect like God. And the knowledge of the mystery of death coupled with the indwelling of the Holy Spirit leads to perfect living and the assurance of eternal life. This is the way by which Jesus lived and never sinned. Simply put, the dead do not sin. Thus, righteousness is wrought in death. It was the reason for all the animals being sacrificed in the earthly sanctuary services and eventually for the Lamb of God, Jesus, dying for us.

Those who have relinquished ownership of themselves to God and live by the principle of death, in them is fulfilled the scripture saying: "I am crucified with Christ: nevertheless I live: yet not I, but Christ liveth in me: and the life which I now live in the flesh I live by the faith of the Son of God, who loved me, and gave himself for me. I do not frustrate the grace of God: for if righteousness come by the law, then Christ is dead in vain" (Gal. 2:20-21 KJV)

It is by the principle of death that Jesus lived and never sinned. His senses were dead to sin. He lived moment by moment as one who was dead to sin but alive unto righteousness. Living as one who is dead to sin but alive unto righteousness, he lived by the principle of baptism. Jesus also lived every day of his life as his last day and as such he lived by the principle of the last day, the seventh day, which has death as its principle. Living every day as his last day, he did not work the work of sin and therefore he enjoyed perfect peace and rest which are also principles of the seventh and last day.

In culmination of the principle by which he lived Jesus died on the cross for our observation besides the means for our salvation. Therefore, those who will follow in the example of Jesus, will live every day of their lives as their last day and moment by moment as the dead. They will also cease from the work of sin and enter the rest, peace and bliss of God. Thus, living by the principles of the Sabbath day, they will live all the days of their lives in a Sabbath rest.

Death is a principle and a weapon. The principle and weapon which will destroy Satan is death. For this reason, Jesus came to the earth and died. So, says the scripture: "Forasmuch then as the children are partakers of flesh and blood, he also himself likewise took part of the same; that through death he might destroy him that had the power of death, that is, the devil (Heb. 2:14 KJV)

Like the Captain of our salvation who became victorious over Satan through death, everyone who seeks to be victorious over Satan, sin and self, must be armed with the weapon which destroys these three, which is death. The principle of death is cessation from sin, and the weapon of death is to destroy sin. In death, sin is rendered powerless. When you are armed with death, you disarm Satan when he tempts you and with his own weapon you destroy him.

Every temptation, therefore, is to be countered with these three words, "I am dead." By so doing the follower of Christ puts the frame of his mind in the state of the dead. As you do this, God also sees and acknowledges your desire to die to sin and he empowers you with his Holy Spirit to dissipate the temptation. This is how Jesus lived and never sinned, and this is what it means to, "deny yourself, pick up your cross daily and follow him."

It is in living by the principles of death and the last day that we shall be victorious over every sin. To this end the apostle Paul counsels, saying:

> There is therefore now no condemnation to them which are in Christ Jesus, who walk not after the flesh, but after the Spirit. For the law of the Spirit of life in Christ Jesus hath made me free from the law of sin and death. For what the law could not do, in that it was weak through the flesh, God sending his own Son in the likeness of sinful flesh, and for sin, condemned sin in the flesh. That the righteousness of the law might be fulfilled in us, who walk not after the flesh, but after the Spirit. For they that are after the flesh do mind the things of the flesh; but they that are after the Spirit the things of the Spirit. For to be carnally minded is death;

but to be spiritually minded is life and peace. Because the carnal mind is enmity against God: for it is not subject to the law of God, neither indeed can be. So, then they that are in the flesh cannot please God. But ye are not in the flesh, but in the Spirit, if so be that the Spirit of God dwell in you. Now if any man have not the Spirit of Christ, he is none of his. And if Christ be in you, the body is dead because of sin; but the Spirit is life because of righteousness. But if the Spirit of him that raised up Jesus from the dead dwell in you, he that raised up Christ from the dead shall also quicken your mortal bodies by his Spirit that dwelleth in you. Therefore, brethren, we are debtors, not to the flesh, to live after the flesh. For if ye live after the flesh, ye shall die: but if ye through the Spirit do mortify the deeds of the body, ye shall live. For as many as are led by the Spirit of God, they are the sons of God. (Romans 8:1-14 KJV)

Those who live by the principle of death have applied the atoning blood of the Lamb of God to their hearts. They are like the children of Israel who had the blood of the Passover lamb sprinkled on their doorposts. And in the night when the Lord passed through Egypt none in their homes were destroyed. The destroying angel passed over them. But those who lack the knowledge of the mystery of death, and do not live by the principle of death, shall be destroyed by death. They shall be like the Egyptians who did not know to understand why the children of Israel had the sprinkling of the blood of the Passover lamb on their doorposts. And in the night of the Passover when the destroying angel passed through Egypt there was a great cry in the homes of the Egyptians.

The greatest discovery in the whole universe is the science of the cross, for it is in this that we learn to become like the Most High God. Everyone who seeks to be like God in character must be like the apostle Paul who said: "For I determined not to know anything among you, save Jesus Christ, and him crucified." (1 Cor. 2:2 KJV) The apostle Paul again wrote to the church at Corinth and said, "I protest by your rejoicing which I have in Christ Jesus our Lord, I die daily." (1 Corinth. 15:31 KJV)

The principle by which God lives is death to sin thus his dying for the identification and observation of his person and character to be made known throughout the universe. And everyone who desires to be like God must live by the principle of death to sin. This includes Lucifer whose desire and famous cry is, "I will be like the Most High!"

The only way to be like the most High is to die to sin. So, in the end, those who died to sin shall be exalted to live like the most High but those who lived unto sin shall be humbled to die and in death become like God who does not sin.

It is about time for Lucifer to have his hearts' desire, for the secret of how to be like the Most High has now been revealed unto all intelligent beings. Let everyone, both men and angels stand in awe of the Great and Wonderful God. For if God had just destroyed Lucifer without an explanation who would have understood God and the meaning of death. But for every intelligent being to come to the knowledge that what Lucifer had desired to have in heaven when he said, "I will be like the Most High," and ever since his rebellion he has been fighting to be like the Most High, only for it to be revealed that the way to be like the Most High, is death, and it is also the weapon that will destroy Lucifer, is a thing so amazing. I stand amazed!

Since the dwelling place and sanctuary of God is in the seventh and last day, if Lucifer wants to be like the Most High, he must come to the dwelling place of God which is the last day and there to become like God. And everyone who enters the dwelling place of God enters the place of death and must die. You either die by baptism to enter the sanctuary of God or wait to die eternally on the day of the Lord's appearing, at the last day.

Since Lucifer wants to be like the Creator, though he is a creature, he must like the Creator bring his work to an end. In the end, at the last day, Lucifer will bring his work of the creation of sin to an end and he will become like God who ended his creation on the seventh and last day of the week and entered the Sabbath rest from his works.

It is in this place, the seventh day, in a moment, at the last day, when at last Lucifer will learn to be like the Most High when he shall bring his work to an end and like the dead take a rest from his works. In this place, Satan, sin and all those who lived unto self, seeking to be first all the time will become the last, for they would have come to the place of last.

In this place, the last day, Lucifer, this troubled angel who used to be in the sanctuary of God but went out in search of how to be like the Most High, will at last in the last day find where and how to be like the Most High. The place to be like God is in his sanctuary, the seventh day, and how to be like God are in the unchangeable principles of the seventh day, which are last, death and rest and which defines the character of God found in death to sin. The psalmist says, "Thy way O God, is in the sanctuary" (Psalm 77:13 KJV) And here, in the sanctuary of God, everyone who seeks to know God and to be like him must come to gain the knowledge to be like God and to experience how to be like God. Those who go into the sanctuary of God by choice, will live like God. But those who will wait to be taken there, will die and in death become like God who does not sin.

The way to be like God, therefore, are in the principles of the sanctuary. And those who seek to be like God will live every day of their lives as their last day on earth, the day of death. They have ceased from sin and have entered rest. Also, in their dealings with their fellow men, those who live as the dead will choose to be last in everything. Therefore, those who will find this secret way, the seventh day, and the treasure of knowledge there, and want it for themselves, upon them is pronounced a blessing. The prophet John in vision seeing those who choose dying to sin to be their lot says: "And I heard a voice from heaven saying unto me. 'Write, Blessed are the dead which die in the Lord from henceforth: Yea, saith the Spirit, that they may rest from their labors; and their works do follow them." (Rev. 14:13, KJV)

Satan does not want anybody to know the truth about the seventh day, because its principles are the weapons for every child of God to defeat him and they are the weapons by which God will destroy him and sin. Through the ages, and especially from the period of time known in history as the dark ages, and unto the present time, Satan has worked hard to deceive many to believe that the Lord's Day is Sunday the first day of the week. Beginning with the Emperor Constantine who in the year 321 A.D. decreed that Sunday become a holy day, Satan has supplanted God's holy day, the seventh and *last* day (which has embedded in it the principles to living the perfect life), with the *first* day of the week which alludes to the principles of self and self-worship.

Evangelicals, giving the reason why they observe Sunday as the Lord's Day, says, "Since Jesus resurrected on the first day of the week, Sunday has become the Lord's Day." But there is no record of this in the scriptures and there is no record saying, "the Lord blessed and sanctified the First day," as he did the seventh day at the end of the creation week. The reason for observing Sunday, the first day of the week, given by the Evangelicals as the Lord's Day, is Satan's lie.

The day which the Lord calls his holy day is the seventh day which is recorded in the bible. In the counsel of God on how to observe the Sabbath day, God describes the Sabbath day as, *"my holy day"* and *"the holy of the Lord."* Speaking about how to observe his holy day, the Lord says:

> If thou turn away thy foot from the Sabbath, from doing thy pleasure on *my holy day*; and call the Sabbath a delight, *the holy of the Lord*, honorable; and shalt honor him, not doing thine own ways, nor finding thine own pleasure, nor speaking thine own words: Then shalt thou delight thyself in the Lord; and I will cause thee to ride upon the high places of the earth, and feed thee with the heritage of Jacob thy father: for the mouth of the Lord hath spoken it (Isaiah 58:13-14 KJV)

Satan in seeking to deceive the world into destruction, has taken advantage of many for their lack of knowledge and understanding of the scriptures, to misconstrue certain parts of the scriptures. One of such scriptures, is to be found in Paul's epistle to the Colossians where he talks about certain ordinances which has been taken away, being nailed to the cross when Jesus died. Paul speaks to the Colossians saying: "And you, being dead in your trespasses and the uncircumcision of your flesh, he has made alive together with him, having forgiven you all trespasses, having wiped out the handwriting of requirements that was against us, which was contrary to us. And he has taken it out of the way, having nailed it to the cross. Having disarmed principalities and powers, he made a public spectacle of them, triumphing over them in it. So let no one judge you in food or in drink, or regarding a festival or a new moon or Sabbaths, which are a shadow of things to come, but the substance is of Christ." (Col. 2:13-17 NKJV)

In Paul's epistle, he refers to the ceremonial laws of ordinances given to the children of Israel by God, and which had in them many days celebrated as Sabbath days by the children of Israel. These Sabbath days are embodied in that part of the ceremonial laws called the "Feasts of the Lord." These festivals which are described and listed in Leviticus chapter twenty three, are: The seventh day Sabbath, the Passover and Unleavened Bread, the Feast of Firstfruits, the Feast of Weeks, the Feast of Trumpets, the Day of Atonement and the Feast of Tabernacles. However, let us take notice that the Seventh day Sabbath is embodied both in the ceremonial laws of festivals, called the Feasts of the Lord and the moral laws of the Ten Commandments. The Seventh day Sabbath law, the Fourth Commandment, has its perpetuity as part of the moral law, the Ten Commandments, which is God's standard of judgment for the characters of all intelligent beings. If the Seventh day Sabbath had only been a part of the ceremonial laws of the Feasts of the Lord then it would have been abolished together with the other feast days which had days of rest also described as Sabbath days.

Satan has taken advantage of what Paul said to the Colossians to mean that the Seventh day Sabbath has been abolished. This is one of Satan's lies and his greatest deception in the world, because he knows that those who will find the truth about the Seventh day Sabbath and abide by it will defeat him.

Those who are the servants of God live by the principles of the Sabbath day. They choose to be last because they live every day of their lives as their last day on earth. This is the last day people, the seventh day people. Their principle of life is death, which is the principle of the last day, and which is also the principle and purpose of baptism and the power by which to overcome sin.

The reason to be baptized to become a part of the church and body of Christ is to live by the principle of death which is the principle of the last day and the place of the sanctuary of God. Those who discover this truth will worship God on the seventh day and honor the day in commemoration of the principle by which they live. The Sabbath day will become what it is supposed to be for them; "The sign between them and God and that it is God who sanctifies them." (Ezek. 20:12, 20 KJV) They will be identified as the last day people, the seventh day people, as they wait in anticipation of their Lord's return, which will be on the seventh and last day cut off for the salvation of men. These are the people who have become partakers of the Lord's death and have become worshipers in the sanctuary of God.

On the night before the Lord Jesus died, he celebrated the Lord's supper with his disciples. The scripture, says:

> And as they were eating, Jesus took bread, and blessed it, and brake it, and gave it to the disciples, and said, Take, eat; this is my body. And he took the cup, and gave thanks, and gave it to them, saying, Drink ye all of it; For this is my blood of the new testament, which is shed for many for the remission of sins. But I say unto you, I will not drink henceforth of this fruit of the vine, until that day when I drink it new with you in my Father's kingdom. (Matt. 26:26-29 KJV)

The apostle Paul referred to the Lord's supper and said: "For I have received of the Lord that which also I delivered unto you, That the Lord Jesus the same night in which he was betrayed took bread: And when he had given thanks, he brake it, and said, Take, eat: this is my body, which is broken for you:  this do in remembrance of me. After the same manner also he took the cup, when he had supped, saying, this cup is the new testament in my blood: this do ye, as oft as ye drink it, in remembrance of me. For as often as ye eat this bread, and drink this cup, ye do show the Lord's death till he come." (1 Cor. 11:23-26, KJV)

In his gospel message, the Lord Jesus invites everyone who is burdened with sin to come unto him for rest. He says: "Come unto me, all ye that labour and are heavy laden, and I will give you rest. Take my yoke upon you, and learn of me; for I am meek and lowly in heart: and ye shall find rest unto your souls. For my yoke is easy, and my burden is light." (Matt. 11:28-30 KJV) This gospel message of Jesus, is an analogy, using the account of the creation week of the six days in which God worked and the seventh day in which he rested. The keywords in the scripture are *labor, heavy laden, yoke, burden* and *rest*. The invitation of the Lord Jesus to all those who *labor* and are *heavy laden*, to come unto him for *rest*, is an invitation to sinners who have *worked* in their lifetime the *work* of sin, to come unto him for *rest*. The place where Jesus is inviting them to come for *rest*, is the sanctuary of God, the resting place of God, where they can be baptized and partake of the death of Christ. Therefore, the sanctuary and its ordinances all have one principle, which is death.

In the earthly sanctuary, the altar of burnt sacrifices which was in the outer court of the sanctuary, symbolized the death of Jesus. The laver, also in the outer court, in which the priests washed their hands and feet, and which symbolized baptism, has its principle as death. The table of shewbread in the holy place of the sanctuary, from which the priests ate every Sabbath, also symbolized the broken body of Christ, the Bread of Life, for the children of God. The altar of burnt incense, also in the holy place symbolized the sacrifice of prayer where confession and the forsaking of sin is made. The seven golden candlesticks which symbolized the church and every child of God as light, is effectual because the "Light of the world" had to pass through death and darkness so sinners could receive his light. The ministration of the high priest in the most holy place by the atoning blood of the Lord's goat, also symbolized the ministration of Christ our High Priest with the atoning blood of, "the Lamb of God, which taketh away the sin of the world." (John 1:29 KJV)

The Lord God has declared, and it is the only way, that the salvation of man would be through the shedding of blood. He declares the only way to salvation by saying, "For the life of the flesh is in the blood: and I have given it to you upon the altar to make an atonement for your souls: for it is the blood that maketh an atonement for the soul." (Lev.

17:11 KJV) Again, the word of God says: "And almost all things are by the law purged with blood; and without shedding of blood is no remission." (Heb. 9:22 KJV)

Everyone who comes to the place of the sanctuary of God must first observe and accept the death of Christ at the cross for himself and agree in a covenant with God through baptism to die to sin in like manner as Christ died for him. When a person shall do this, he is then ready to enter the sanctuary to become a member of the royal priesthood of God and to partake in the ordinances of the sanctuary which are all rooted in death. But those who do not heed the invitation of Jesus and do not partake of the Lord's death shall taste of death at the appearing of the Lord. This is what Jesus referred to when he said to the children of Israel, "Verily I say unto you, that there be some of them that stand here, which shall not taste of death, till they have seen the kingdom of God come with power." (Mark 9:1 KJV)

There comes the day when Satan and all those who lived unto sin will come to the place of the sanctuary of God, the seventh day, and there, they will die. Their place of burial which will be their baptism is hell. In this place sin and sinners will perish and they will not rise again.

Many in Christendom are observing Sunday the first day of the week, as the Lord's Day. This is the greatest deception in the history of mankind and the history of the churches. By this deception Satan is holding the supposedly churches of God captive that they may not experience the fullness of the Spirit of God working in them.

Since the creation of the earth, God has divided the history of the earth into segments of a seven-day cycle. The first segment of the seven-day cycle began with the creation of the earth on the first day and ended on the seventh day at the end of God's creative work. The cycle has continued ever since the creation week. Of the many segments of the seven-day cycle that has passed since the creation of the earth, the last day of the history of the earth and of sin, will fall on the last day of the last segment of the seven-day cycle. Simply, the history of the earth began on the first day of the week and the end of the history of the earth will fall on the last day of the week, which will be no other day but the seventh day, the day of completion and perfection.

As God ended his creative work on the seventh day of the first segment of the seven-day cycle, in like manner the history of the earth will end with the end of the work of every man on the last day of the last segment of the seven-day cycle. In that day, every man will rest from their works at the appearing of the Lord of the Sabbath day. Those who lived by dying to sin will resurrect to become the first but those who lived unto sin will die to become the last and enter rest.

It is the work of Satan that men may not know the truth about the seventh day because by the knowledge and application of the principles of the seventh day they shall be victorious over every temptation. The reason being that the dead are irresponsive to anything and you cannot arouse the dead to sin. So, when in our minds we die to sin, then just like Jesus cried on the cross, "It is finished," then all is finished between us and our enemy. We can therefore be victorious over Satan only when we make the seventh day and its principles the sanctuary in which we dwell and our fortress against the assault of sin.

The last and final day of the experience with sin is fast approaching. When the prophet John was banished to the Isle of Patmos, God revealed to him events of the last days and what will signal the end of the salvation message of God and to usher in the last day. It was shown in vision to John seven angels blowing seven trumpets. It was also shown to him that at the sounding of the seventh trumpet, the mystery of God should be finished. John writes saying: "But in the days of the voice of the seventh angel, when he shall begin to sound, the mystery of God should be finished, as he hath declared to his servants the prophets." (Rev. 10:7, KJV) As the seven angels blow their trumpets, the seven angels with the vials of the wrath of God will pour out their vials upon the earth. When the seventh angel pours out his vial into the air, God shall declare from heaven saying, "It is done." The apostle John who saw these things in vision says: "And the seventh angel poured out his vial into the air, and there came a great voice out of the temple of heaven, from the throne, saying, 'It is done.'" (Rev. 16:17 KJV)

Just as Jesus cried out on the cross saying, "It is finished," at the end of his sacrificial ministry when he gave himself as an offering for the remission of sins, (and when he cried thus, it was the eve of the

Sabbath day) God will cry out from heaven to declare the end of his saving grace by saying, "It is done." This will end the history of this world of sin and signal the eternal death to sin and its perpetrators at the last day. When this happens, it will be the outworking of the principle of the last day, to usher in eternal holiness and righteousness, as holiness and righteousness are wrought in death.

The history of the wickedness of this world and its final destruction is symbolized by the story of the fall of Jericho. Jericho that wicked city was overthrown miraculously by the power of God after the children of Israel have marched around it for seven days. And on the seventh day, the priests and the soldiers marched around the city seven times blowing their trumpets and the walls of Jericho tumbled down. The account of the fall of Jericho is recorded in Joshua chapter six.

The symbols in the story of Jericho are a representation of what is going on in this present wicked world. Jericho represents the world. The priests who carried the ark of the testament represent those who are showing to the world that we are to fear God and keep his commandments. The priests marching around Jericho seven times also represent the children of God who are sounding the gospel message around the world until the last day and when the seventh trumpet should sound in heaven. Rahab the harlot also represents all sinners who hear the gospel message and believe, that they may not be destroyed with the world. The piece of red cloth, which Rahab hang on the side of her building, as a sign between her and the children of Israel, which saved her and her household, represent the blood of Jesus Christ which saves us from our sins.

Just as the walls of Jericho fell at the sounding of the seventh trumpet, the blowing of the seventh trumpet in heaven by the seventh angel will bring this wicked world to an end. This will culminate in the end of the gospel message which is symbolized by the priests of Israel blowing their trumpets on the seventh day as they marched around the walls of Jericho. So, says the Lord Jesus, "And this gospel of the kingdom shall be preached in all the world for a witness unto all nations; and then shall the end come." (Matt. 24:14 KJV) That last day will be on the seventh and last day of the week when this wicked world shall be overthrown by the power of God at the sounding of the trumpet by the archangel, and the Lord shall appear to take his ransomed home with him to heaven. So the apostle Paul says: "For the Lord himself shall descend from heaven with a shout, with the voice of the archangel, and with the trump of God: and the dead in Christ shall rise first: Then we which are alive and remain shall be caught up together with them in the clouds, to meet the Lord in the air: and so shall we ever be with the Lord. Wherefore comfort one another with these words." (1 Thess. 4:16-18, KJV)

In the end of time there will be two resurrections rightfully called the first and second resurrections. The first resurrection will be at the appearing of Jesus at the last day which God has put in his own power to bring the mystery of sin to an end. This resurrection is reserved for those who chose to be last by dying to sin as they lived. All those who have died believing in Christ shall resurrect first to become "the first," together with those who never died but lived by the principle of death to sin. They shall resurrect to be "the first" and to live unto righteousness forevermore.

The second resurrection will be after the period of the millennium of Christ's appearing. This will be after the saints have reigned a thousand years in heaven with Christ. At the end of the thousand years, Jesus will descend with the Holy City, the New Jerusalem, the bride of the Lamb which is the church and ransomed of the earth. As they descend to the earth, God will make all the wicked to resurrect. This is the second resurrection. They shall resurrect only to be destroyed with Satan and his angels in the lake of fire and they shall be punished with the second death to be "the last" which is eternal death.

The apostle John in vision talks about the events that will happen during and after the thousand years, saying:

> And I saw an angel come down from heaven, having the
> key of the bottomless pit and a great chain in his hand.
> And he laid hold on the dragon, that old serpent, which
> is the Devil, and Satan, and bound him a thousand
> years. And cast him into the bottomless pit, and shut
> him up, and set a seal upon him, that he should deceive

the nations no more, till the thousand years should be fulfilled: and after that he must be loosed a little season. And I saw thrones, and they sat upon them, and judgment was given unto them: and I saw the souls of them that were beheaded for the witness of Jesus, and for the word of God, and which had not worshipped the beast, neither his image, neither had received his mark upon their foreheads, or in their hands; and they lived and reigned with Christ a thousand years. But the rest of the dead lived not again until the thousand years were finished. This is the first resurrection. Blessed and holy is he that hath part in the first resurrection: on such the second death hath no power, but they shall be priests of God and of Christ, and shall reign with him a thousand years. And when the thousand years are expired, Satan shall be loosed out of his prison. And shall go out to deceive the nations which are in the four quarters of the earth, Gog and Magog, to gather them together to battle: the number of whom is as the sand of the sea. And they went up on the breadth of the earth, and compassed the camp of the saints about, and the beloved city: and fire came down from God out of heaven and devoured them. And the devil that deceived them was cast into the lake of fire and brimstone, where the beast and the false prophet are, and shall be tormented day and night for ever and ever. And I saw a great white throne and him that sat on it, from whose face the earth and the heaven fled away, and there was found no place for them. And I saw the dead, small and great, stand before God, and the books were opened: and another book was opened, which is the book of life: and the dead were judged out of those things which were written in the books, according to their works. And the sea gave up the dead which were in it: and death and hell delivered up the dead which were in them: and they were judged every man according to their works. And death and hell were cast into the lake of fire. This is the second death. And whosoever was not found written in the book of life was cast into the lake of fire." (Rev. 20:1-15, KJV)

When these things shall be accomplished, "the last" shall become "the first" in the first resurrection, and "the first" shall become "the last" in the second and last resurrection only to be punished with the second death, which is eternal death.

# GOD'S SEAL OR SATAN'S MARK

The Seventh day and the holiness of God are the seals of God. In the end of his created works, God sealed his creation with the Seventh day. The Seventh day is like the seal of a manufacturer who places his seal on his products to identify them as made by him. The fourth commandment, the Sabbath law, is therefore the stamp of God's authority as the Author and Creator of the heavens, the earth, the seas and all things in them. Thus, in giving the reason why the Sabbath is to be honored and kept holy, God says: "Remember the Sabbath day to keep it holy.... For in six days the Lord made heaven and earth, the sea, and all that in them is, and rested the seventh day: wherefore the Lord blessed the Sabbath day, and hallowed it." (Exod. 20:8-11 KJV)

God's holiness is the seal upon the seal of the seventh day Sabbath. In the end of his creation, God clothed and covered his created works with his holiness as he breathed his Spirit over his created works and the seventh day. The ending act of God in his creation says: "Thus the heavens and the earth were finished, and all the host of them. And on the seventh day God ended his work which he had made; and he rested on the seventh day from all his work which he had made. And God blessed the seventh day, and sanctified it: because that in it he had rested from all his work which God created and made." (Gen. 2:1-3 KJV)

Also, in the redemption of man, the Sabbath commandment as the seal of God, is the sign between God and his people, that he is the God who sanctifies them; which means he is the God who sets them apart as holy. God speaks saying, "Moreover I also gave them my Sabbaths, to be a sign between them and me, that they might know that I am the Lord who sanctifies them." (Ezek. 20:12 NKJV) God also gives counsel to his people about the Sabbath, that the keeping of the Sabbath is the acknowledgment of him as the Lord our God. So, he says: "Hallow my Sabbaths, and they will be a sign between me and you, that you may know that I am the Lord your God." Ezek. 20:20 NKJV)

The seventh day Sabbath, also as a sign of the sanctification and cleansing act of God, is the day in which God wants to have an intimate relationship with his people. The kind of intimate relationship that God would like to have with his people is the relationship of a husband and a wife.

At the end of the creation week, the thing that God blessed besides blessing the seventh day, was the marriage between Adam and Eve. The marriage between Adam and Eve was to symbolize the marriage relationship between God and his people. The Apostle Paul wrote and said:

"Husbands, love your wives, even as Christ also loved the church, and gave himself for it; that he might sanctify and cleanse it with the washing of water by the word, that he might present it to himself a glorious church, not having spot, or wrinkle, or any such thing; but that it should be holy and without blemish. So ought men to love their wives as their own bodies. He that loveth his wife loveth himself. For no man ever yet hated his own flesh; but nourisheth and cherisheth it, even as the Lord the church: For we are members of his body, of his flesh, and of his bones. For this cause shall a man leave his father and mother, and shall be joined unto his wife, and they two shall be one flesh. This is a great mystery: but I speak concerning Christ and the church. Nevertheless let every one of you in particular so love his wife even as himself; and the wife see that she reverence her husband." (Ephesians 5:25-33 KJV)

As on the first Sabbath day of creation when God blessed the marriage of Adam and Eve, in like manner on every Sabbath day God wants to relate to us as our husband, and with us as his bride. It is the time that God wants us to present ourselves before him as his bride, and everyone of his people, personally, as the one he has chosen to be his bride.

As the bride will wear her white spotless garment to be married to her bridegroom, so on the Sabbath day the Lord will like his bride to wear her white garment, the robe of righteousness. This garment of righteousness is the garment which the Lord himself has given to his bride through sanctification. The prophet Isaiah prophesied about Israel, saying: "I will greatly rejoice in the LORD, my soul shall be joyful in my God; for he hath clothed me with the garments of salvation, he hath covered me with the robe of righteousness, as a bridegroom decketh himself with ornaments, and as a bride adorneth herself with her jewels." (Isaiah 61:10 KJV)

Every Sabbath day is a wedding day and a rehearsal day towards the great wedding day when the Lamb of God will be married to his bride. Everyone who will get himself ready, will be counted as one of the wise virgins in Jesus' parable of the five wise and five foolish virgins.

The white garment, the robe of righteousness, which the bride of Christ is to wear, is the law of God. The law is to be worn as a garment. It is this garment of God which has no spot or wrinkle. When a person wears the law as a garment, it manifests him as wearing the spotless and perfect character of God as a garment. But those who do not wear the law as a garment, are naked. Thus, Adam and Eve saw that they were naked after they sinned. Before they sinned, Adam and Eve were clothed with the law, the garment of light which covers God, and which is the presence of Christ as the image of God. Therefore, the Lord is warning the children of the earth, saying: "Behold, I come as a thief. Blessed is he that watcheth, and keepeth his garments, lest he walk naked and they see his shame." (Revelation 16:15 KJV)

Throughout eternal ages, the garment of light, the law, will be the garment that the righteous will wear. That garment of light which covers God, and which is the presence of Christ as Light, will be the garment that covers the righteous. They will wear Christ as a garment and the sanctuary in which they dwell.

So, the day is coming, when all the righteous shall sit at the welcome table of the Lord, to sup with him, at the marriage feast of the Lamb of God and his bride. The apostle John who was made to see that day in vision, wrote and said:

"And I heard as it were the voice of a great multitude, and as the voice of many waters, and as the voice of mighty thunderings, saying, Alleluia: for the Lord God omnipotent reigneth. Let us be glad and rejoice, and give honour to him: for the marriage of the Lamb is come, and his wife hath made herself ready. And to her was granted that she should be arrayed in fine linen, clean and white: for the fine linen is the righteousness of saints. And he saith unto me, Write, blessed are they which are called unto the marriage supper of the Lamb. And he saith unto me, these are the true sayings of God." (Revelation 19:6-9 KJV)

In the end of his creation, as God sealed his created works with the seventh day, he empowered them with the principles of the seventh day and enabled them to the obedience of those principles by sealing them with the power of his Holy Spirit. Yet God gave to Adam and Eve the freedom to choose to obey him or to do their own will when he gave them the commandment about the tree of the knowledge of good and evil.

When Adam and Eve sinned, they broke the seals of God from them. As the selfless principles of the seventh day were broken from them, Adam and Eve began to live selfishly and to be lawless. The Holy Spirit, the power of God which indwelt them and enabled them to be holy was withdrawn from them. With God's Holy Spirit withdrawn from them, the spirit of Satan came in as a rushing wind, took possession of them and inhabited them.

As the spirit of Satan inhabited Adam and Eve the whole human race was corrupted with sin and became the possession of Satan since all generations of humanity were in the loins of Adam and Eve when they sinned. Therefore, the apostle Paul says: "Wherefore, as by one man sin entered into the world, and death by sin, and so death passed upon all men, for that all have sinned." (Rom. 5:12 KJV) This means in the loins of Adam all were corrupted by sin and death passed upon all men.

In the temptation in the garden of Eden, Satan issued commands and suggestions contrary to the command of God and led Eve and Adam to reject God as their God and to set themselves up as their own gods. After creating Adam and Eve, the word of God says: "And the Lord God commanded the man, saying, 'Of every tree of the garden you may freely eat; but of the tree of the knowledge of good and evil you shall not eat, for in the day that you eat of it you shall surely die.'" (Gen. 2:16 NKJV) But the Serpent in his discourse with Eve, countered the express command of God with his opposing command and suggestion to Eve saying to her: "You will not surely die. For God knows that in the day you eat of it your eyes will be opened, and you will be like God, knowing good and evil." (Gen. 3:4 NKJV)  This act of issuing commands and suggestions contrary to the commands and statutes of God, which in the beginning led Adam and Eve to reject God as the God to be worshiped and obeyed, and which in turn resulted with them setting themselves up as their own gods, is what amounts to the mark of Satan, which is also the mark of the beast.

The mark of Satan when applied is self-worship. Self-worship is following the dictates of one's own mind and not adhering to the commandments of the Creator. When in heaven, Lucifer decided to ascribe worship to himself and not to give allegiance to the God who created him, he claimed for himself what is due God alone. On the contrary, the seal of God has to do with obedience to the commandments of God which expresses the selfless character of God. So, in the end, it will be said of those who keep the commandments of God: "Here is the patience of the saints; here are those who keep the commandments of God and the faith of Jesus." (Rev. 14:12 NKJV)

The mark of Satan is manifested through pride, self-exaltation and mounting the throne in one's heart as God. It was Lucifer who first rebelled against God through pride, self-exaltation and in seeking to mount the throne of God to be worshiped as God. In heaven, Lucifer intimated to himself saying: "I will ascend into heaven, I will exalt my throne above the stars of God: I will sit also upon the mount of the congregation, in the sides of the north: I will ascend above the heights of the clouds: I will be like the most High." (Isa. 14: 13-14 KJV)

In his rebellion, Lucifer led some of the angels of heaven to rebel with him, and they have all received the mark of Satan in worshiping Satan. The apostle John in vision speaks about the breakout of the rebellion of Satan and the angels who followed in his folly, saying: "And there was war in heaven: Michael and his angels fought against the dragon: and the dragon fought and his angels, and prevailed not; neither was their place found any more in heaven. And the great dragon was cast out, that old serpent, called the Devil, and Satan, which deceiveth the whole world: he was cast out into the earth, and his angels were cast out with him." (Rev. 12:7-9 KJV)

Since the mark of Satan which is also the mark of the beast is in setting aside the commandments of God, it is therefore the usurping of the authority of God and supplanting another as god who should be obeyed. The authority of God is in his word and commandments. Therefore, whosoever issues a law or a commandment to be obeyed in place of the commandments of God usurps the authority of God and sets himself up as the god to be obeyed.

In the Garden of Eden, the Serpent, which here was the beast and medium through which Satan worked, usurped the authority of God and set himself up as the one to be obeyed. Satan in seeking to bring the whole creation of God to worship him introduced the mark of the beast to Adam and Eve when he said to Eve through the serpent(beast), saying: "For God doth know that in the day ye eat thereof, then your eyes shall be opened, and ye shall be as gods, knowing good and evil." (Gen. 3:5 KJV) By eating the fruit of the knowledge of good and evil, Adam and Eve obeyed the Serpent instead of the expressed command of God, and they sinned.

As the mark of the beast is in issuing commands or suggestions contrary to the commandments and statutes of God, it is therefore also living in accordance with the dictates of one's own will in opposition to the commandments of God. When you live according to the dictates of your own will, you make for yourself your own set of commandments contrary to the commandments of God. It can therefore be summed up in one word, and that word is sin. The apostle John says: "Whosoever committeth sin transgresseth also the law: for sin is the transgression of the law." (1 John 3:4 KJV) And everyone who sins has the mark of the devil. Thus, the apostle John continue to say: "He that committeth sin is of the devil; for the devil sinneth from the beginning..." (1 John 3:8 KJV)

Anything that is accounted as sin, opposes the commandments of God, and seeks to exalt itself above the commandments of God and to supplant them. So therefore, "the beast" who opposes God is called, "the man of sin." Speaking about some of the events that should precede the coming of the Lord Jesus Christ, the apostle Paul wrote and said: "Let no one deceive you by any means; for that Day will not come unless the falling away comes first, and *the man of sin* is revealed, the son of perdition, who opposes and exalts himself above all that is called God or that is worshiped, so that he sits as God in the temple of God, showing himself that he is God." (2 Thess. 2:3-4 NKJV)

The mark of the beast is in the example of what the devil did in the beginning by setting aside the law of God and putting himself in the place of God. Therefore, anyone who persists in sin acquires the title, "In Place of God," which is also the title of the beast. Those who persists in sin are living out the mindset of Satan when he said in heaven, "I will be like the Most High," and later in the Garden of Eden when he said to Eve, "You will be like God." So those who continue in sin want to sit on the throne like God, but they do not want his character.

When you decide to do anything contrary to the will of God, you declare yourself your own god. In effect you practice the mark of the beast by exalting your will above the will of God. This is what the devil did in the beginning in heaven and it is what Adam and Eve did in the Garden of Eden. It is also what the beast has done.

The people of the earth today are practicing the mark of the beast. Because the children of the earth are living in disobedience to the commandments of God and have made themselves their own gods, the first angel in the vision of the prophet John, begins his message, saying: "Fear God and give glory to Him, for the hour of His judgment has come; and worship Him who made heaven and earth, the sea and springs of water." (Rev. 14:7 NKJV)

The knowledge of the seal of God is to encourage the children of God to keep the commandments of God and to be holy. But the knowledge of the mark of the beast is to serve as a deterrent to the children of God to keep them away from sinning. So, the wise man Solomon gives counsel and warns, saying: "Let us hear the conclusion of the whole matter: Fear God, and keep his commandments: for this is the whole duty of man. For God shall bring every work into judgment, with every secret thing, whether it be good, or whether it be evil." (Eccl. 12:13-14 KJV) The third angel in the vision of John also warns the people of the earth of the consequence of worshiping the beast, saying:

> If any man worship the beast and his image, and receive his mark in his forehead, or in his hand, the same shall drink of the wine of the wrath of God, which is poured out without mixture into the cup of his indignation; and he shall be tormented with fire and brimstone in the presence of the holy angels, and in the presence of the Lamb: And the smoke of their torment ascendeth up for ever and ever: and they have no rest day nor night, who worship the beast and his image, and whosoever receiveth the mark of his name. (Rev. 14:9-11 KJV)

What is at stake, that Satan contends with God over the souls of men? These bodies that we possess which God made to be his sanctuary and dwelling place, Satan also wants it for himself that he may indwell us and live out his life of sin through us. So, for example, when Cain killed Abel, it was Satan indwelling Cain through his spirit, who killed Abel who had the Spirit of God in him. And when David laid with Bathsheba, Satan entered David, and through David, Satan together with David laid with Bathsheba.

In whatever we do, it is either the Spirit of God or the Spirit of Satan working in us for good or evil. Therefore, the apostle Paul says: "And you He made alive, who were dead in trespasses and sins, in which you once walked according to the prince of the power of the air, *the spirit who now works in the sons of disobedience*, among whom also we all once conducted ourselves in the lusts of our flesh, fulfilling the desires of the flesh and of the mind, and were by nature children of wrath, just as the others." (Eph. 2:1-3 NKJV)

So, in this struggle between God and Satan over the souls of men, the question to be answered by every person, which also will result in the choices we make, is: "Who will you have to indwell you; God or Satan?" If we choose God, he will live out his life in us through his Spirit to keep his commandments, and we will have his seal upon us. But if we choose Satan, he will live out his life of sin and lawlessness in us and we will have his mark upon us.

In his contention over the souls of men, Satan seeks to displace God from indwelling us that he will come in place of God to live in us. The battle, therefore, is over the sanctuary and dwelling place of God and the principles through which the sanctuary is established.

Since the fall of man, Satan has led many to follow in the example of the Serpent to lead people and nations away from worshiping the Creator God. King Nebuchadnezzar usurped the authority of God when he built an image of gold and heralded unto all people to worship his golden image. The marriage of King Ahab to Jezebel a heathen woman also led Israel into apostasy. Jezebel introduced the worship of Baal to Israel until on Mount Carmel when the Lord answered the prayer of Elijah by fire, did the people say, "The Lord he is the God, the Lord, he is the God." (1 kings 18:39 KJV) Elijah had earlier said to the people, saying: "How long halt ye between two opinions? If the Lord be God, follow him: but if Baal then follow him." (1 Kings 18:21 KJV)

Since the fall of man, the history of humanity has been marked with the worship of idols. Anybody or anything we exalt above the Creator becomes our god and idol. It is the will of Satan that people worship anybody or anything other than the Creator. So, through the ages, Satan has led the children of the world to devise systems of worship for themselves. People today are worshiping idols rather than to worship the Creator through the form of worship He has designed for His worship. This is another form of the mark of Satan and the mark of the beast.

Any system of worship which men have devised and are worshiping through it, gives practice to the mark of the beast. They are the systems of the mark of the beast because they do not profess the commandments of God and the testimony of Jesus Christ. Therefore, if any desire to worship God, they must come to the place of His sanctuary, and acquire the knowledge for the worship of the Creator.

The knowledge of God and his will is in His commandments which was deposited in the ark of the testament in the most holy place of the sanctuary. And the will of God is that his created beings keep his commandments. Wherefore the wise man Solomon says: "Let us hear the conclusion of the whole matter: Fear God and keep His commandments: for this is the whole duty of man." (Eccl. 12:13, KJV) Jesus also says: "If ye love me keep my commandments." (John 14:15, KJV) However the original error of Lucifer, the originator of sin was in setting aside the commandments and principles of God and imposing his will above the will of God.

The mark of Satan therefore is in imposing his will above the will of God. When you impose your will above the will of God you make for yourself your own law to govern your life and you become your own god. By persisting in your own will, you desire to preserve and protect your chosen lifestyle, and if it were possible, to save it unto life everlasting. But all who choose to keep safe their own chosen lifestyles and not submit to the will of God will lose it. Therefore, whosoever will live by his own will, and not submit to the will of God, is in effect receiving the mark of Satan which is also the mark of the beast. The word of God says: "He that committeth sin is of the devil; for the devil sinneth from the beginning." (1 John 3:8, KJV)

The controversy between God and Satan is about who is to be worshiped. It has been the intent of Satan to wrestle the rule of the whole creation from the Creator. This contention which Satan started in heaven has been carried to the earth. His strategy has been to issue commands and suggestions contrary to the laws and commands of God.

Since God cast him out of heaven, Satan has not relented in his effort to wrestle the rule of the whole creation from God. The temptation of Jesus in the wilderness was another attempt of Satan to wrestle the sovereignty of the universe from the Creator. In seeking to bring the Creator under his power and dominion, Satan issued commands to Jesus subtly veiling them in suggestions. If Jesus had obeyed any of the suggestions Satan issued to him, he would have come under the power and authority of Satan. This would have resulted in worship of Satan. Moreover, Jesus who is God, would have surrendered the dominion of the universe to Satan as Adam and Eve gave up the dominion of the earth when they obeyed the voice of Satan.

In the temptation in the wilderness, the first two suggestions of Satan to Jesus were cleverly veiled to hide their real intent. But in his madness and desperation when he was unsuccessful with his usual craft of deceit, Satan spoke openly and asked the Creator to worship him. In his ambition for the Creator to worship him, Satan offered to give to Jesus what he was seeking to wrestle from him. Consumed with an envy for worship, Satan imagined the unthinkable, that he a created being should seek worship from the Creator.

Satan's unrelenting ambition is that he should be worshiped as God. Thus, when he tempted Jesus to worship him, Jesus countered him and said, "Get thee hence, Satan: for it is written, thou shalt worship the Lord thy God, and him only shalt thou serve." (Matt. 4:10, KJV)

In his contention with God for worship, Satan has chosen to supplant the commandments of God with sin. Armed with sin, he warred in heaven against God and the angels who remained loyal to God. He continues his battle for worship on earth with the weapon of sin. The battle for the supremacy on earth is between the laws of God and sin. Therefore, Satan is angry with those who keep the commandments of God.

The apostle John in vision prophesies about the end times of the struggle between good and evil and how Satan will fight against those who keep the commandments of God. John says: "And the dragon was wroth with the woman, and went to make war with the remnant of her seed, which keep the commandments of God, and have the testimony of Jesus Christ." (Rev.12:17 KJV) It is in this prophecy, that we see the fulfilment of the promised prophecy of God in the beginning of the struggle between good and evil, when God said to the Serpent, "And I will put enmity between you and the woman, and between your seed and her Seed; He shall bruise your head, and you shall bruise His heel." (Gen. 3:15 KJV) This war between Christ and Satan, which was decided at the cross with the fate of Satan, continues to be waged between Satan and the remnant of the seed of the woman; those described as the ones "who keep the commandments of God and have the testimony of Jesus Christ." (Rev. 12:17 KJV)

Since Satan carried this war against God to the inhabitants of the earth, he has always been seeking for men to exalt themselves as gods to be worshiped. The apostle Paul prophesied that before the day of the Lord comes, Satan will lead somebody to manifest himself in the temple of God that he is God. This person or persons who will take on this role will be so exalted among men as the Father to be called Papa which in the Greek language, is Abba. The apostle Paul prophesies and says: "Let no man deceive you by any means: for that day shall not come, except there come a falling away first, and that man of sin be revealed, the son of perdition: who opposeth and exalteth himself above all that is called God, or that is worshipped; so that he as God sitteth in the temple of God, shewing himself that he is God." (2 Thess. 2:3-4 KJV)

Also, God made our bodies to be his temple and dwelling place. So, the apostle Paul says: "What? Know ye not that your body is the temple of the Holy Ghost which is in you, which ye have of God, and ye are not your own?" (1 Cor.6:19 KJV) Since God made our bodies to be his temple, if we allow God to dwell in us, we worship God. But those who deny God from dwelling in their bodies take the temple of God to be their own and worship themselves. Thus, those who deny God from dwelling in them, come after the nature of "the man of sin and son of perdition," who as God sits in the temple of God showing himself that he is God. In effect, until those who have taken possession of themselves as their own, surrender themselves to God, they have the stamp of the mark of the beast and Satan on them.

The apostle Paul in his prophecy about the end of those who oppose God and exalt themselves as God, says: "And then shall that Wicked be revealed, whom the Lord shall consume with the spirit of his mouth, and shall destroy with the brightness of his coming: Even him, whose coming is after the working of Satan with all power and signs and lying wonders, and with all deceivableness of unrighteousness in them that perish; because they received not the love of the truth, that they might be saved." (2 Thess. 2:8-10 KJV)

The last act of Satan in his struggle for worship will be to set up a system of worship to oppose the worship of God and to deceive the world. This system of worship will be difficult for many to discern its deceptiveness because it will be called a church of God and it will mix truth with error. Satan will give great authority to the men who will occupy the seat as head of this false church, by letting them assume the titles and attributes of God that they may be worshiped as God.

The apostle John was made to prophesy about the rise of this false system of worship, and it was symbolized as a beast. John in his prophesy says:

> And I stood upon the sand of the sea, and saw a beast rise up out of the sea, having seven heads and ten horns, and upon his horns ten crowns, and upon his heads the name of blasphemy. And the beast which I saw was like unto a leopard, and his feet were as the feet of a bear, and his mouth as the mouth of a lion, and the dragon gave him his power, and his seat, and great authority. And I saw one of his heads as it were wounded to death; and his deadly wound was healed: and all the world wondered after the beast. And they worshipped the dragon which gave power unto the beast: and they worshipped the beast, saying, who is like unto the beast? Who is able to make war with him? And there was given unto him a mouth speaking great things and blasphemies; and power was given unto him to continue forty and two months. And he opened his mouth in blasphemy against God, to blaspheme his name, and his tabernacle, and them that dwell in heaven. And it was given unto him to make war with the saints, and to overcome them: and power was given

him over all kindred, and tongues, and nations. And all that dwell upon the earth shall worship him, whose names are not written in the book of life of the Lamb slain from the foundation of the world. (Rev. 13:1-8 KJV)

The head of this false church, "the beast," is the same one that the apostle Paul makes mention of, saying: "The man of sin, the son of perdition, who opposeth and exalteth himself above all that is called God, or that is worshipped." (2 Thess. 2:3-4 KJV) It was also given to the prophet Daniel to prophesy about this same "beast" who will make war with the saints of God and seek to change the laws of God. The prophet Daniel in his prophecy says: "And he shall speak great words against the most High, and think to change times and laws: and they shall be given into his hand until a time and times and the dividing of time." (Dan. 7:25 KJV)

This false church with its head symbolized as a beast has since the prophecy of John, "risen" among the nations. Since its foundation, it has transferred the observance of the Sabbath, (God's law which deals with time) from the seventh day to the first day. In transferring the solemnity of the Sabbath from the seventh day to the first day the claim is made by this false church that since Jesus resurrected on the first day, the first day has become the new Sabbath and the Lord's day. But the reason God gives for the observance of the Sabbath is the creation and not the resurrection, although especially important in God's salvation plan.

The Sabbath is for all creation to acknowledge God as the Creator and as a day of rest as God rested from his works in the very beginning of creation. This is the significance of the first angel's message as he warns the inhabitants of the earth by invoking the fourth commandment, saying: "Fear God and give glory to Him, for the hour of His judgment has come; and worship Him *who made heaven and earth, the sea and springs of water.*" (Rev. 14:7 NKJV)

Attempting to change God's law which deals with God's time for worship, this false church has fulfilled the prophecy of Daniel, where he says, "he shall think to change times and laws". This therefore identifies this false church as the "beast" whose mark is assuming to change the laws of God. By issuing a law contrary to the law of God to be in place of one of the laws of God which deals with time, this "beast" power has done just like the Serpent did when he deceived Eve in the garden of Eden. Through this deception, men are obeying the beast rather than God.

John the revelator in his prophecy said that this beast shall be wounded but his wound shall be healed. And in the very end of time, another beast shall rise who shall cause all people to worship the first beast. John continues his prophecy saying:

> And I beheld another beast coming up out of the earth; and he had two horns like a lamb, and he spake as a dragon. And he exerciseth all the power of the first beast before him, and causeth the earth and them which dwell therein to worship the first beast, whose deadly wound was healed. And he doeth great wonders, so that he maketh fire come down from heaven on the earth in the sight of men. And deceiveth them that dwell on the earth by the means of those miracles which he had power to do in the sight of the beast; saying to them that dwell on the earth, that they should make an image to the beast, which had the wound by a sword, and did live. And he had power to give life unto the image of the beast, that the image of the beast should both speak, and cause that as many as would not worship the image of the beast should be killed. And he causeth all, both small and great, rich and poor, free and bond, to receive a mark in their right hand, or in their foreheads: And that no man might buy or sell, save he that had the mark, or the name of the beast, or the number of his name. Here is wisdom. Let him that hath understanding count the number of the beast: for it is the number of a man: and his number is six hundred threescore and six. (Rev. 13:11-18 KJV)

As revealed in the prophecy of John, the beast is a man. Therefore, it is for every person who seeks the knowledge and understanding of God to find and identify the man who is the beast. The mark of the beast is in choosing the first day of the week which has been passed into law as the Lord's day, in place of the seventh day which is the Lord's day. The name of the beast is Father or Papa (Pop), as he chooses to sit in the temple of God showing himself like God. The number of the beast is also the number which can be counted in one of his names and titles and which adds up to 666. The title translates to mean in English, "In place of the Son of God."

The seal of God, the seventh day Sabbath law, identifies the Creator as the Maker of the heavens, the earth, the seas and all that are in them. The seal of God therefore makes known his domain of authority. The mark of the beast in contrast identifies the beast as the one who has supplanted the seal of God with the first day. By claiming the first day to be the Lord's day, it makes it his mark exercising authority over the creation of God. By this deception, many professed Christians have been deceived into believing that the first day is the Lord's day instead of God's definitive seal and day of worship.

The prophet John standing on the Isle of Patmos was made to prophesy about the end times, how God will send messengers with warnings to warn the inhabitants of the earth against receiving the mark of the beast. John in vision says:

> And I saw another angel fly in the midst of heaven, having the everlasting gospel to preach unto them that dwell on the earth, and to every nation, and kindred, and tongue, and people, saying with a loud voice, fear God, and give glory to him; for the hour of his judgment is come: and worship him that made heaven, and earth and the sea, and the fountains of waters. And there followed another angel, saying, Babylon, is fallen, is fallen, that great city, because she made all nations drink of the wine of the wrath of her fornication. And the third angel followed them, saying with a loud voice, if any man worship the beast and his image, and receive

his mark in his forehead, or in his hand, the same shall drink of the wine of the wrath of God, which is poured out without mixture into the cup of his indignation; and he shall be tormented with fire and brimstone in the presence of the holy angels, and in the presence of the Lamb: And the smoke of their torment ascendeth up forever and ever: and they have no rest day nor night, who worship the beast and his image, and whosoever receiveth the mark of his name. (Rev. 14:6-11 KJV)

The first angel calls for all people, nations, tongues and kindred to the worship of God. Embedded in his message is the wording of the fourth commandment, the seal of God, as he calls all people to worship, "*him that made heaven, and earth, and the sea, and the fountains of waters.*" Therefore, the first angel's message is a call to all people to acknowledge God as their Creator and to have his seal, the seventh day Sabbath law, upon them.

The second angel's message symbolizes the beast as Babylon. Why Babylon? Why does God employ the name of Babylon in the prophecy because Babylon had ceased to exist as a nation at the time God gave this prophecy to John. Babylon, in the vision of John, is a symbol of the Babylonian Empire under the rule of Nebuchadnezzar. It was Nebuchadnezzar who made a huge golden image and asked all people to worship it. The book of Daniel says:

Nebuchadnezzar the king made an image of gold, whose height was sixty cubits and its width six cubits. He set it up in the plain of Dura, in the province of Babylon. And King Nebuchadnezzar sent word to gather together the satraps, the administrators, the governors, the counselors, the treasurers, the judges, the magistrates, and all the officials of the provinces, to come to the dedication of the image which King Nebuchadnezzar had set up. So the satraps, the administrators, the governors, the counselors, the treasurers, the judges, the magistrates, and all the officials of the province gathered together for the dedication of the image that King Nebuchadnezzar had set up; and they stood before the image that Nebuchadnezzar had set up. Then a herald cried aloud: 'To you it is commanded, O peoples, nations, and languages, that at the time you hear the sound of the horn, flute, harp, lyre, and psaltery, in symphony with all kinds of music, you shall fall down and worship the gold image that King Nebuchadnezzar has set up; and whoever does not fall down and worship shall be cast immediately into the midst of a burning fiery furnace.' So at that time, when all the people heard the sound of the horn, flute, harp and lyre, in symphony with all kinds of music, all the people, nations, and languages fell down and worshiped the gold image which King Nebuchadnezzar had set up. (Dan. 3:1-7 NKJV)

In Nebuchadnezzar's time, Babylon was the ruling world empire. In fact, history has it that Babylon was the first world empire. As such Babylon had its king, Nebuchadnezzar, as the king of the world. In other words, he was the king of all the kings in the world, and he is rightfully called king of kings in the Bible. The prophet, Daniel, revealing and interpreting the dream of Nebuchadnezzar, which dream had gone away from the king after he dreamed it, said to the king: "You, o king, are a king of kings. For the God of heaven has given you a kingdom, power, strength, and glory" (Dan. 2:37 NKJV). But there is another who is King of kings of the universe, and that is Jesus. When the apostle John saw Jesus in a vision, as the Commander of the armies in heaven, he says: "And he has on his robe and on his thigh a name written: King *of kings and Lord of lords*" (Rev. 19:16 NKJV).

When God showed to Nebuchadnezzar in a dream using the illustration of a huge image of man, with the head of gold, the breast and arms of silver, the belly and thighs of brass, the legs of iron and the feet of part iron and part clay, God made it known to Nebuchadnezzar that his kingdom will pass away and another and still others will follow till the kingdom of God shall be established which kingdom shall not pass away. But Nebuchadnezzar set up a huge image of gold from head to toe implying that his kingdom, which was represented by the head of gold in the dream of God, will stand forever. By this act Nebuchadnezzar challenged the word of God.

The king of the world had set his throne as the god of the world by demanding from men what to worship. It was Satan, the god of this world and the one who opposes God, who had spoken through Nebuchadnezzar to set up the image and cause all men to worship it.

The message of the herald of Babylon is identical to the message of the first angel of John's vision. Both call all people, nations, and languages into worship. The difference, though, is that, while the first angel calls all people into the worship of God, the herald of Babylon calls all people into the worship of an image. Therefore, the message of the herald of Babylon stands in direct opposition to the message of the first angel. As the first angel preaches the everlasting gospel of God, he casts down the adulterous message of the herald of Babylon, with which Nebuchadnezzar had sought to win the affection and allegiance of all men, throughout all time.

The third angel's message says:

> If any man worship the beast and his image, and receive his mark in his forehead, or in his hand, the same shall drink of the wine of the wrath of God, which is poured out without mixture into the cup of his indignation; and he shall be tormented with fire and brimstone in the presence of the holy angels, and in the presence of the Lamb: And the smoke of their torment ascendeth up for ever and ever: and they have no rest day nor night, who worship the beast and his image, and whosoever

receiveth the mark of his name. Here is the patience of
the saints: here are they that keep the commandments
of God, and the faith of Jesus. (Rev. 14:9-12 KJV)

The message of the third angel is also identical to the message of the herald of Babylon. Both talk about the consequences of not obeying the command they bear. Those who did not obey the command of the herald of Babylon were to be punished by being cast into a burning fiery furnace. And those who do not obey the command given by the first angel will be punished with fire and brimstone. Since the third angel gives a warning against worshipping the beast and his image and the reception of his mark, these must stand in direct opposition to the worship of God and the sign of God.

Like Babylon of old under the rule of king Nebuchadnezzar, who commanded that all people, and nations and languages worship his image of gold, the false church will ask that all people *universally* become a part of the church. But when the first angel begins to call all people to acknowledge God as their Creator and to have the seal of God upon them, he causes this new Babylon to fall, as those who hear his message and obey it, come out of Babylon to the worship of the true God with their acceptance of God's seal upon them. This leads the second angel to cry out, "Babylon is fallen, is fallen, that great city, because she made all nations drink of the wine of the wrath of her fornication." The false church, the new Babylon, make the nations "drunk" with her concoction of truth and error by which she has an illicit relationship with them.

The third angel's message speaks of the consequence of worshiping the beast and his image and of receiving his mark. Like the herald of Babylon, who spoke of the consequence of not worshiping the golden image of king Nebuchadnezzar as being cast into a fiery furnace, the third angel also speaks of the consequence of worshiping the beast, as having upon you the wrath of God, which is poured out without mixture into the cup of his indignation with the torment of fire and brimstone.

The messages of the three angels are to call forth all people to come out of the worship of the beast unto the worship of God.

After hearing the messages of the three angels, the apostle John says then he heard another voice from heaven, speaking unto him, saying: "Write, blessed are the dead which die in the Lord from henceforth: Yea, saith the Spirit, that they may rest from their labours; and their works do follow them." (Rev.14:13 KJV). This voice from heaven carries a double message. First, it speaks of those who have departed this life and have died in the Lord. In death they have ceased from their works and have entered rest. Secondly, it speaks of those who, though living, live as though they are dead and, therefore, have entered the Sabbath rest of God. The apostle Paul says: "For ye are dead, and your life is hid with Christ in God. When Christ who is our life, shall appear, then shall ye also appear with him in glory" (Col. 3:3-4 KJV).

In these last days, God is calling all people to come out of this false church which he also calls Babylon the great. The apostle John in his visions was made to see another angel who cries out with a loud voice to the inhabitants of the earth to come out of Babylon the great. He says:

> And after these things I saw another angel come down from heaven, having great power; and the earth was lightened with his glory. And he cried mightily with a strong voice, saying, Babylon the great is fallen, is fallen, and is become the habitation of devils, and the hold of every foul spirit, and a cage of every unclean and hateful bird. For all nations have drunk of the wine of the wrath of her fornication, and the kings of the earth have committed fornication with her, and the merchants of the earth are waxed rich through the abundance of her delicacies. And I heard another voice from heaven, saying, come out of her, my people, that ye be not partakers of her sins, and that ye receive not of her plaques. For her sins have reached unto heaven, and God hath remembered her iniquities. (Rev. 18:1-5 KJV)

The wine of the wrath of the fornication of Babylon the great, is the mixture of truth and error in her hands, by which, like wine that intoxicates and confuses the mind, she makes the nations drunk. The kings of the earth also commit fornication with Babylon the great, by their allegiance to the beast.

God is in these last days sealing in the minds of those who heed his warning with his seals, before the day of his appearing. In the very same way as he covered his creation with the seals of the seventh day and his Holy Spirit at the end of his creative work, God is covering his servants with his seals in the end of his salvation work.

The apostle John was made to see in vision, the angels of God, holding the winds of strife, till the servants of God are sealed. John says:

> And after these things I saw four angels standing on the four corners of the earth, holding the four winds of the earth, that the wind should not blow on the earth, nor on the sea, nor on any tree. And I saw another angel ascending from the east, having the seal of the living God: and he cried with a loud voice to the four angels, to whom it was given to hurt the earth and the sea, saying, hurt not the earth, neither the sea, nor the trees, till we have sealed the servants of our God in their foreheads. (Rev. 7:1-3 KJV)

The apostle Paul also speaks about the seal of the Holy Spirit upon those who believe the gospel of Jesus Christ, saying: "In him you also trusted, after you heard the word of truth, the gospel of your salvation; in whom also, having believed, you were sealed with the Holy Spirit of promise, who is the guarantee of our inheritance until the redemption of the purchased possession, to the praise of his glory." (Ephesians 1:13-14 NKJV)

The death of Jesus Christ is the greatest lesson for all of God's created and intelligent beings on how to be like God in character. And the seal of God, the seventh and last day, which has last, death and rest as its principles, is the way to be like God. In contrast Satan who has desired to be like God seeks to be first in everything. In seeking to be first,

Satan does not want to die to self, but to live unto self. As he seeks to be first, Satan lives by covetousness and selfishness.

The day set aside by man, which has no scriptural basis or authority, which men are observing in opposition to God's expressed sign, is the mark of the beast. The whole issue is about whom are we going to worship and obey. God or Satan? The seventh day Sabbath, the last of the days of the week—God's sign to sanctification, which is perfect and holy living and the way to love, which is laying one's life down for others and for God and choosing to be the *last* in all things—or the *first* day of the week, which makes manifest self and the "*Me first*" idea of Satan.

The seal of God, therefore, is the imprint of self-denial in the minds of those who have relinquished ownership of themselves to God, to become His new creatures. On the contrary, the mark of the beast is the imprint of self-centeredness in the minds of those who do not choose to surrender their lives to God, and for that reason have become their own gods.

The symbol of the seal of God is the Sabbath, the seventh and *last* day of the week, and its principle is self-denial, which results in faith in God. In like manner, the symbol of the mark of the beast is Sunday, the *first* day of the week, and its principle is self-dependence.

The mark of the beast, therefore, is found in gratifying self and not in pleasing God. Those who live unto self, have made themselves their own gods. Therefore, all who live to gratify self are receiving the mark of the beast which is also the mark of Satan. The first day of the week, which has first as its principle, symbolizes the selfish and covetous character of Satan. All who choose the first day as the Lord's day are receiving the mark of Satan which is also the mark of the beast and the mark of self.

The day of the Lord, the last day, is fast approaching. And in that day, many from one end of the earth to the other will perish. Men, women, boys and girls will perish in that day. They will perish because they did not receive the seal of God over his creation though they were created by God. And they will perish because they did not have the principles of the seal of God sealed in their minds as the principles by which they lived. Having lived by the principle of being first, they will in that last day die, as the principle of the seal of God is holiness, which is wrought in death. Moreover, they will perish because they did not accept the rebirth of the soul through the blood of Jesus Christ and regeneration by the Holy Spirit. The Lord Jesus says himself: "For God so loved the world, that he gave his only begotten Son, that whosoever believeth in him should not perish, but have everlasting life." (John 3:16, KJV) Again Jesus says: "Verily, verily, I say unto thee, except a man be born of water and the Spirit, he cannot enter into the kingdom of God." (John 3:5 KJV)

Those who receive the salvation of God, are like the children of Israel who lived in Egypt in bondage to Pharaoh, and God sent the deliverer, Moses, to deliver them. On the night of their deliverance they were saved by the blood of the Passover lamb. Their last day in Egypt was the day they were set free from bondage and God gave them rest from their hard labor in Egypt. In giving them rest, God gave them his commandment and sign as a memorial of their deliverance from bondage and slavery. God's commandment to the children of Israel says: "Keep the Sabbath day to sanctify it, as the LORD thy God hath commanded thee. Six days thou shalt labour, and do all thy work: But the seventh day is the Sabbath of the LORD thy God: in it thou shalt not do any work, thou, nor thy son, nor thy daughter, nor thy manservant, nor thy maidservant, nor thine ox, nor thine ass, nor any of thy cattle, nor thy stranger that is within thy gates; that thy manservant and thy maidservant may rest as well as thou. And remember that thou wast a servant in the land of Egypt, and that the LORD thy God brought thee out thence through a mighty hand and by a stretched out arm: therefore the LORD thy God commanded thee to keep the Sabbath day." (Deut. 5:12-15 KJV)

In like manner God is coming to save his children from bondage to the "Pharaoh" of this world, Satan, who has put the inhabitants of the world to the hard labor of sin. The day is coming when those who cry unto the Lord and have put their trust in the saving grace of God will be set free forever from the power and rule of the taskmaster of sin. The Passover sacrifice for their deliverance has already been made. So, the scripture says: "So Christ was once offered to bear the sins of many; and unto them that look for him shall he appear the second time without sin unto salvation." (Heb. 9:28 KJV)

In that last day God will send the Deliverer from sin, the Son of God, to deliver his children from the world of sin. In that day, all those who have the blood of Jesus covering them, will be set free forever, and God will give them rest.

The Sabbath will be a perpetual celebration through eternal ages, as a memorial to the children of God for their deliverance from bondage and slavery to sin. Thus, the Lord says, through the prophet Isaiah: "For as the new heavens and the new earth, which I will make, shall remain before me, saith the Lord, so shall your seed and your name remain. And it shall come to pass, that from one new moon to another, and from one Sabbath to another, shall all flesh come to worship before me, saith the Lord." (Isaiah 65:22-23 KJV)

In the day of the Lord, when Christ shall appear, those who will be living and will be translated without seeing death, will be only those who keep all of the commandments of God and notably the seventh day Sabbath with its principles of last, death and rest which in turn are the principles of perfection in character. In that day of the Lord, none who do not keep the Sabbath holy shall be translated without seeing death. For the Lord will come in his holy day and only those who would have entered his sanctuary and dwelling place to be part of his sanctuary would have made themselves ready by having the seal of God to go to heaven with him.

As the Lord will come in his holy day, the last day, to bring the work of every man to an end, there will be a re-enactment of the Fourth Commandment, which says: Remember the Sabbath day, to keep it holy. Six days you shall labor and do all your work, but the seventh day is the Sabbath of the Lord your God. In it you shall do no work: you, nor your son, nor your daughter, nor your male servant, nor your female servant, nor your cattle, nor your stranger who is within your gates. For in six days the Lord made the heavens and the earth, the sea, and all that is in them, and rested the seventh day. Therefore the Lord blessed the Sabbath day and hallowed it." (Exod. 20:8-11, NKJV) In that day all those who will be found not keeping this commandment will be found guilty in disobedience to the commandment. The consequence for disobeying the Fourth commandment is death as death is its principle; and those who will die will bring their work to an end.

In the end, those who will find the principles of the last day, and live by them, and observe the Sabbath, would have found the secret to being like God. Righteous living and perfection in character are wrought in death and in dying to sin. The dead do not sin. Therefore, to have the mental disposition of the dead and live every day as the last day like the dead who have entered the last day of their time on earth, is the secret way to be perfect in character like God.

Jesus says the day of the Son of man will be like the days of Noah. In the days of Noah, God instructed Noah to build an ark and everyone who went into the ark was safe from the flood. In like manner, in the day of the Lord's appearing, God's "ark of safety" will be the seventh and last day, the place of refuge from sin. For he will come in his holy day at the completion of his salvation work. And all those who would have made the last day their dwelling place and place of refuge will be safe from the rain of fire that is to rain on the earth. But those who would not have lived to make the last day their dwelling place will be consumed by the fire of God. So, the apostle Paul says: "Since it is a righteous thing with God to repay with tribulation those who trouble you, and to give you who are troubled rest with us when the Lord Jesus is revealed from heaven with his mighty angels, in flaming fire taking vengeance on those who do not know God, and on those who do not obey the gospel of our Lord Jesus Christ. These shall be punished with everlasting destruction from the presence of the Lord and from the glory of his power, when he comes, in that day, to be glorified in his saints and to be admired among all those who believe, because our testimony among you was believed." (1 Thess. 1:6-10 NKJV)

The gospel of Jesus Christ and the truth about the Sabbath is being preached unto all men. And this is the last call of God to all people of the earth to come into his "ark of safety," the seventh day Sabbath, before he comes to destroy the earth with the rain of fire. So, he warns the earth saying, "But as the days of Noah were, so also will the coming of the Son of man be. For as in the days before the flood, they were eating and drinking, marrying and giving in marriage, until the day that Noah entered the ark, and did not know until the flood came and took them all away, so also will the coming of the Son of man be." (Matt. 24:37-39 NKJV)

Those who will live unto the day of the Lord and survive the rain of fire will be those who would have entered God's "ark of safety" for the last day. The seventh day Sabbath is God's "ark of safety" because it is the place in time for the worship of God and the place of refuge and hiding place from the assault of sin.

Since the inception of sin, the tempest of sin has been raging on earth. The only hiding place from the tempest of sin is in death. Sin has no power and dominion over the dead. So, unless the inhabitants of the earth by trusting in God live as though they are dead, they will all be swept away by the tide of sin. Therefore, it is only those who will hide themselves in death and live in the context and defines of the last day as their hiding place, shall arise to live forever when the storm of sin shall pass by.

The power to overcome sin is death. Therefore, those who will be overcomers will be only those who will arm themselves with death and trust in the death of Jesus for the remission of their sins. They would have died to sin themselves through living by the principles of death and arising to live forevermore in righteousness; death to sin but alive unto righteousness, these two things which are the principles of baptism, gives entrance into the sanctuary and kingdom of God. The apostle John prophesies about those who will be overcomers, saying: "Then I heard a loud voice saying in heaven, 'Now salvation, and strength, and the kingdom of our God, and the power of His Christ have come, for the accuser of our brethren, who accused them before our God day and night, has been cast down. And they overcame him by the blood of the Lamb and by the word of their testimony, and they did not love their lives to the death." (Rev. 12:10-11 NKJV)

In the end, there is a word which will destroy Satan. That word which will destroy Satan is the word, LAST. When the principle of the word LAST, which is to be the last, shall be fulfilled in Satan, this king of fools will become the last and die. For behold time is rushing on like a rushing wind, to bring Satan to that place, the last day, where he will be made the last. This place is the dwelling place of God and all who enter that place must die to sin. In this place, the last day, Satan and all those who continued in sin will die. For in the place of last there is no sin, and all who get to the place of last do not sin.

The seventh and last day of the week is not a day arbitrarily chosen by God to be the Sabbath day. But the seventh and last day of the week is the Sabbath day because of its principles which generates life and holiness. Those who obey its principles will live, but those who disobey its principles, that same principles will destroy them.

In the end those who will arise to live forever will be those who would have lived as though they were dead. Having lived by the principles of death, they surrendered their bodies to God, that Christ, manifesting himself as the Holy Spirit, should be the one living in them. In so doing, their bodies become the place housing the Spirit of God. This act will complete the building of God's heavenly sanctuary. In that day will be the fulfillment of the prophecy, saying: "Behold, the tabernacle (sanctuary) of God is with men, and he will dwell with them, and they shall be his people. God himself will be with them and be their God." (Rev.21:3 NKJV) This prophecy interprets to mean, "the dwelling place of God is with men, and he will dwell with them, and they shall be his people." This is so, because they would have made themselves to be a sanctuary for God to dwell in them.

This act will be the fulfillment of the antitype of the instruction God gave to Moses, when he told him to tell the children of Israel, saying: "And let them make me a sanctuary; that I may dwell among them." (Exod. 25:8 KJV) The real and true sanctuary of God is built with the principles of the seventh day, the Sabbath day, and the people of God.

Just like God told the children of Israel in the time of Moses, saying, "And let them make Me a sanctuary, that I may dwell among them," in the end, all those who surrendered themselves to God, will be the lively stones used in building up the sanctuary of God, for an indwelling of His Spirit. It is to this end that the apostle Paul wrote and said, "Now, therefore, you are no longer strangers and foreigners, but fellow citizens with the saints and members of the household of God, having been built on the foundation of the apostles and prophets, Jesus Christ

Himself being the chief cornerstone, in whom the whole building, being fitted together, grows into a holy temple in the Lord, in whom you also are being built together for a dwelling place of God in the Spirit." (Eph. 2:19-22 NKJV)

The people who make up the building and sanctuary of God are built up by the principles of the last day, the seventh day, and their dwelling place is the seventh day. Therefore, the seventh day is the place where God's sanctuary is erected and assembled. To sum it up, the place of the sanctuary of God is the seventh day and the worshipers of God who are the lively stones built up by the principles of the seventh day, altogether make up the sanctuary of God.

The attempt to transfer the solemnity of the seventh day to the first day is Satan's attempt to cast down and destroy the place and sanctuary of God and the worshipers of God. This has been Satan's way of getting a host of people and drawing worship to himself in the churches by deceiving the people that the first day is the new Sabbath and the Lord's day because the Lord resurrected on that day. By supplanting the seventh day with the first day, Satan seeks to supplant the principles of the sanctuary which are all rooted in death, with the principles of being alive to sin.

Satan has plotted to undermine the laws of God in the churches, that the unsuspecting and ignorant people of the earth will accept the laws of the deceiver as the laws of God which will cost them the loss of their souls. Therefore, the warning of God comes to the people of the earth and to any who shall accept the transfer of the Sabbath from the seventh day to the first day which is the mark of the beast, saying: "If anyone worships the beast and his image, and receives his mark on his forehead or on his hand, he himself shall also drink of the wine of the wrath of God, which is poured out full strength into the cup of his indignation. He shall be tormented with fire and brimstone in the presence of the holy angels and in the presence of the Lamb. And the smoke of their torment ascends forever and ever; and they have no rest day or night, who worship the beast and his image, and whoever receives the mark of his name." (Rev. 14:9-11 NKJV) But those who keep the commandments of God in truth, God says of them through the prophet John saying: "Here is the patience of the saints; here are those who keep the commandments of God and the faith of Jesus. Then I heard a voice from heaven saying to me, Write: 'Blessed are the dead who die in the Lord from now on. Yes, says the Spirit, that they may rest from their labors, and their works follow them.'" (Rev.14:12-13 NKJV)

In these last days, God is calling all who have been deceived to accept the mark of the beast and are honoring the first day in the churches as the Lord's day, to come out of "Babylon." To everyone who seeks to worship God in truth, come out from honoring the first day, Sunday, as the Lord's day, to the worship of God on the Sabbath day, and in honor of Him as the Creator and Redeemer of the world.

This is the end time message of God for the end of the world. And this message is all summed up in one word, which is LAST and which is the principle of the last day--to be the last. The earth is soon to enter her eternal Sabbath rest from all her troubles. And those who would see and acknowledge God's sign and live by it will be those who will live to enter God's eternal rest in His kingdom.

# APPLYING THE SECRET

The character of God stands in a marked contrast to the character of Satan. The character of God is to be found in self-denial and the character of Satan in selfishness. It is only the living who have wants and needs. The dead have need of nothing and are mindful of nothing. The man who is seeking to be like Jesus will live a life of self-denial, which will free him from all covetousness and all the cares of this life.

Those who seek to be like God will live by the principle of being last in everything. In all their dealings with their fellow men, they will not seek the first place but the last, because living as the dead, they have no portion in the things of the earth and like the dead they do not seek to be first in anything. Also, having the mental disposition of the dead they will live every moment of their time on earth as their last day, the day of death.

The dead do not seek for the supremacy, neither do they seek to be seen as the greatest, nor do they seek to be popular and famous. For being dead, they are hidden in the grave away from the sight of the living and they lie in humility. Thus, those who would live as the dead, will not seek for the supremacy or to be seen as the greatest, and they will not seek popularity or fame. But rather, those who live as the dead, live in the spirit of humility.

Seeking the supremacy, or to be the greatest, or seeking popularity or fame in any endeavor of life, manifests self-exaltation and the "I must sit on the throne" idea of Lucifer. And to those who engage themselves in self-exaltation in any form, there comes the day when they will die, never to be seen among the living again. That day will be their last day and their last time.

The dead do not hurt in anything. It is only the living who hurt one another. If we should condition our minds to be as the dead, we will not hurt in anything. This will enable us with the power of the Holy Spirit to abide by the commandments of God.

Those who would be like God will cease from their works and enter rest on the seventh and last day of every week as God did after his work of creation. They will honor that day as blessed and set apart by God for holy purpose and they will obey the principles God has given to honor the Sabbath day. By ceasing from their works on the Sabbath day, they will be living by the principles of the dead as the dead who ceased from all their works on their last day and entered rest.

The dead have surrendered the life-giving force which is the spirit to God. Solomon speaking about the state of the dead says: "Then shall the dust return to the earth as it was: and the spirit shall return unto God who gave it" (Eccl. 12:7 KJV). If we are to win the battle against Satan and sin, we are to surrender our lives, like the dead, to God. The apostle Paul, admonishes us, saying: "I beseech you therefore, brethren, by the mercies of God, that you present your bodies *a living sacrifice*, holy, acceptable to God, which is your reasonable service. And do not be conformed to this world, but be transformed by the renewing of your mind, that you may prove what is that good and acceptable and perfect will of God" (Rom. 12:1-2 NKJV). The apostle Paul again counsels, saying: "For if you live according to the flesh you will die; but if by the Spirit you put to death the deeds of the body, you will live" (Rom. 8:13 NKJV).

The truth about us, as men, is that the bodies we possess were not made for us but for God. In other words, we are not our own, but for God. That is, our bodies were made for the indwelling of the Spirit of God, so the invisible God who is a Spirit may be revealed through us. The apostle Paul therefore asks the question: "Or do you not know that your body is the temple of the Holy Spirit who is in you, whom you have from God, and you are not your own?" (1 Cor. 6:19 NKJV).

It is the attempt of Satan to destroy us, by leading us to sin, and in the end destroying the temple of God. The apostle Paul, therefore, cautions us, saying: "Do you not know that you are the temple of God and that the Spirit of God dwells in you? If anyone defiles the temple of God, God will destroy him. For the temple of God is holy, which temple you are" (1 Cor. 3:16-17 NKJV). If we should live with a sense of awareness that the Holy Spirit dwells in us, we will not sin.

The spirit of self which we are to destroy from our lives is the spirit of Satan. Since the fall of man, Satan seeks to indwell the children of men with his spirit of selfishness. And when Satan is in the soul, you become one with his spirit of selfishness, making you who you are, self. With Satan in the soul, your mind comes under his control, and you cannot help yourself but to yield to his promptings to sin. Satan therefore indwells the soul with the desire to sin. So, sin in the soul, is Satan in the soul.

It is Satan who with his indwelling spirit of self, make the hearts of men, "deceitful above all things and desperately wicked." (Jer. 17:9 KJV). When Satan is in the soul, he is in control, and you are out of control. With the control of the minds of men under his power, Satan drives them where he will have them to go, because when he is in the soul, your mind is intertwined with his mind of sin and the good that you want to do, you cannot do.

The mind under the control of Satan is indwelt by Satan and his demons, and the mind is intertwined with their minds. The mind intertwined with the minds of devils, is in bondage to them and you cannot help yourself. It is only when the soul cries out to Jesus for help that the spirit of Satan and his demons are chased out from the soul for Christ to come and indwell the soul with his righteousness. This truth is revealed to us when Jesus met the demoniac. The story of Jesus' encounter with the demoniac, says: "And they arrived at the country of the Gadarenes, which is over against Galilee. And when he went forth to land, there met him out of the city a certain man, which had devils long time, and ware no clothes, neither abode in any house, but in the tombs. When he saw Jesus, he cried out, and fell down before him, and with a loud voice said, what have I to do with thee, Jesus, thou Son of God most high? I beseech thee, torment me not. (For he had commanded the unclean spirit to come out of the man. For oftentimes it had caught him: and he was kept bound with chains and in fetters; and he brake the bands, and was driven of the devil into the wilderness.) And Jesus asked him, saying, what is thy name? And he said, Legion: because many devils were entered into him.  And they besought him that he would not command them to go out into the deep. And there was a herd of many swine feeding on the mountain: and they besought him that he would suffer them to enter into them. And he suffered them. Then went the devils out of the man, and entered into the swine: and the herd ran violently down a steep place into the lake, and was choked. When they that fed them saw what was done, they fled, and went and told it in the city and in the country. Then they went out to see what was done; and came to Jesus, and found the man, out of whom the devils were departed, sitting at the feet of Jesus, clothed, and in his right mind: and they were afraid. They also which saw it told them by what means he that was possessed of the devils was healed. Then the whole multitude of the country of the Gadarenes round about besought him to depart from them; for they were taken with great fear: and he went up into the ship, and returned back again. Now the man out of whom the devils were departed besought him that he might be with him: but Jesus sent him away, saying, return to thine own house, and shew how great things God hath done unto thee. And he went his way, and published throughout the whole city how great things Jesus had done unto him." (Luke 8:26-39 KJV).

Our minds are wired like the wiring in a house to give light, where the electrical current flows through the wires as the power that gives light. We either have the supply of the electrical current flowing through our minds to give light, or, because of sin in the soul have the electrical current cut-off to leave us in darkness and without light. When Jesus who is the Light of life is in the soul, you will be a house of light, with the Holy Spirit who is the electrical current flowing through your mind to give light. But when Satan and sin are in the soul, you will be a house of darkness and death because the source of light is cut off from your soul. And when Christ comes to indwell the soul by invitation, the mind of the person is rewired with the mind of Christ. The Holy Spirit then flows through the wires of the mind of Christ, intertwining the wires of the mind of the person with the wires of the mind of Christ. It is then that the person comes to have the mind of Christ. But if Satan is in the soul, the mind of the person is wired with the mind of Satan and the soul is cut-off from the source of light and Satan will live in the soul with his works of darkness and death.

In his zeal to destroy humans, Satan has commissioned his angels to work in the souls of men to do against the commandments of God. So, Satan and the demons dwell in the souls of men with specific calculated sins to make those sins addictions. There are spirits of whoredoms, spirits of adultery, spirits of fornication, spirits of licentiousness, spirits of lewdness, sprits of lasciviousness, spirits of wrath and hatred, spirits of strife and divisions as seen in wars and competitive sports, spirits of emulation which is competition and includes gambling, spirits of variance with hatred as seen in the politics of the world, spirits of murder, spirits of pride and foolishness, spirits of theft, spirits of lying, spirits of idolatry as manifested in celebrities and movie stars, spirits of witchcraft, spirits of covetousness, spirits of lust, spirits of worrying and murmuring, spirits of gluttony, spirits of gossiping, spirits of foolish jesting, spirits of envying, spirits of reveling, spirits of drunkenness and spirits which work in all works of the flesh. All these sins are the spirits of devils which work in men to manifest themselves in them to the destruction of souls. Every sin that men commit, is the spirit of demons working in them.

To lure humans into sin, Satan has made sin to be put to movies as a form of entertainment, whilst the mind partakes in the display of sins and is constantly fed with the stored-up sins from the recesses of the mind. The men who function as movie stars are the agents and tools of Satan through whom Satan and his demons work to reveal themselves. Those employed as movie stars, worldly musicians and sportsmen who are under the employment of Satan to display all kinds of sin, have unbeknown to them, sold their souls to Satan, in exchange for the high price of money offered them. These people acting as agents and tools of Satan, have a high penalty to pay, in the judgment day of God. In recent modern times, Satan has made sin to be easily accessible to humans, in the palm of their arms, through devices such as the smartphone and the mouse of computers.

Satan is always laying snares for humans. Therefore, Jesus warns those who have received his salvation and have His Holy Spirit indwelling them, not to quench the Holy Spirit from indwelling them, by the neglect of feeding the mind with his word and idleness of an empty mind. Jesus thus warns us, saying: "When the unclean spirit is gone out of a man, he walketh through dry places, seeking rest, and findeth none. Then he saith, I will return into my house from whence I came out; and when he is come, he findeth it empty, swept, and garnished. Then goeth he, and taketh with himself seven other spirits more wicked than himself, and they enter in and dwell there: and the last state of that man is worse than the first. Even so shall it be also unto this wicked generation." (Matt. 12:43-45 KJV).

The apostle Paul admonishes us to bring every thought into captivity to the obedience of Christ. Paul says: "For though we walk in the flesh, we do not war after the flesh: (For the weapons of our warfare are not carnal, but mighty through God to the pulling down of strong holds;) Casting down imaginations, and every high thing that exalteth itself against the knowledge of God, and bringing into captivity every thought to the obedience of Christ; and having in a readiness to revenge all disobedience, when your obedience is fulfilled." (2 Cor. 10:3-6 KJV).

The apostle Paul also encourages those who have become the servants of God, to bring the knowledge of the truth, to those who oppose themselves, and are taken captive by the enemy at his will. Paul speaks, saying: "But foolish and unlearned questions avoid, knowing that they do gender strifes. And the servant of the Lord must not strive; but be gentle unto all men, apt to teach, patient, in meekness instructing those that oppose themselves; if God peradventure will give them repentance to the acknowledging of the truth; and that they may recover themselves out of the snare of the devil, who are taken captive by him at his will." (2 Tim. 2:23-26 KJV).

In his attempt to destroy us Satan has mounted his weapons so sin will be ever present with us. The modern devices like television and computers have become some of the greatest mediums of the weapons of the enemy against the people of this modern age. The movie theatres have also become the church-houses of Satan, where he leads men to defile their souls. Under the guise of entertainment, Satan is making sin attractive from the things shown on television and in the movie theatres. The movies, advertisements and most things shown on television and at the movie theatres, are filled with what the bible identifies as the works of the flesh. The scripture says: "Now the works of the flesh are evident, which are: adultery, fornication, uncleanness, licentiousness, idolatry, sorcery, hatred, contentions, jealousies outbursts of wrath, selfish ambitions, dissensions, heresies, envy, murders, drunkenness, revelries, and the like" (Gal. 5:19-21 NKJV). The movies shown on television and the movie theatres are filled with these things.

The dead do not imagine evil in their minds, neither do they look at the evil imaginations of others made into movies, nor read them in novels; but being dead they have lost their senses of sight and thought. Even the wicked, who in their lifetime loved the world and the things in it, in death lose their sight, and they cannot see those things they loved. If we would be like the dead, who in death have lost their sight, we will put away from our eyes those things which self will like to see. The apostle John, admonishes us, saying:

> Do not love the world or the things in the world. If anyone loves the world, the love of the Father is not in him. For all that is in the world—the lust of the flesh, the lust of the eyes, and the pride of life is not of the Father, but is of the world. And the world is passing away, and the lust of it; but he who does the will of God abides forever. (1John 2:15-17 NKJV)

There is a weapon of the enemy in the world, which works in a seemingly harmless way and is widely displayed in arenas and shown on television around the world. Competitive sports is a powerful weapon of the enemy which destroys men in many ways. The contention for the supremacy, the passion and ambition to be champions, the boisterousness, rowdiness, divisiveness, covetousness, drunkenness, fights and murders, all these works of the flesh which accompany competitive sports, are under the artful scheme of the enemy to destroy souls.

Through competitive sports, Satan sharpens the greatest enemy of man, self, in many, and destroys them. As one man or one team compete against another, self is to be exalted in their quest to prove themselves better than the other. The winners become jubilant, whilst the spirits of the losers are dampened to make them sad. How ungodly! It is never the will of God to make his created beings unhappy in any way.

Those onlookers, the fans who sit back and watch as men contest and duel in sports, are under the spell of demons to take sides so they may desire their favorite to win and to be exalted as better than their opponents. In the end, Satan wants to reproduce his character trait of selfishness, self-exaltation and pride in unsuspecting souls and destroy them. If you have become a child of God and you sit back and watch competitive sports and you take sides, the Spirit of God leaves you because God's Spirit does not indulge in acts of selfish ambition, self-exaltation and hostility.

The spirit of jubilation in those who excel in sports and the spirit of gloom in the losers are not of God but of Satan. The spirit of jubilation in the winners against their opponents manifests love for oneself more than for your neighbor because you would rather, they are down, and you are up. By winning in sports, the winners become proud of themselves. So, competitive sports is a tool of Satan for men to indulge in the spirit of pride. Also, the spirit of gloom which overpower the losers in competitive sports comes from Satan and it is an expression of the failure in the ambition to be exalted and sit on the throne as the greatest.

Those who excel in sports win the admiration of many. If they are men, they are loved by many women, and through this, they are led to indulge in the pleasures of sin; fornication, adultery, reveling, and all other debasing acts. The aim of the master deceiver is to use sports as a tool and mechanism of disguise, to arouse the passions of the heart, to fulfill the lusts of the flesh.

Self-love is idol worship. It is no wonder those who excel in sports are idolized and adored and even worshiped by many. The world sees those who excel in sports as models after whom men are to pattern their lives in the ambition for self-exaltation, whereas the humility and meekness of Jesus is despised.

To compete with anybody for anything is an evil thing and merely the show of self to be seen among the living. For the dead do not compete for anything, neither do they show themselves as better than others in anything. And wherever there is contention and strive, there is no peace. Also, those who pursue fame in any endeavor of life and have become famous, whom men idolize, are being used by Satan as idols to be worshiped.

Another form of evil which works inconspicuously which Satan is using against people in these modern times are the game shows. In America for example, game shows like, "The Price is Right", "Wheel of Fortune", "Jeopardy", "The Pyramid" and "Family Feud", are the weapons of Satan to sharpen selfishness and covetousness in men and to destroy them. Under the guise of entertainment, these programs of the enemy of souls, using subliminal perception, make it appear that what is at stake are some prizes to be won, when what they actually do is arouse covetousness and selfishness in men.

The presentation of awards to movie actors, musicians, models and people in whatever capacity, and to crown who is the best, is of the devil. It is to inspire people to be conformed to his character, that they may feel exalted and to be seen and known as the best, that these programs are set up. The focus in these programs is to see who will be exalted above all others and to be crowned. They all go to manifest the character of Satan, which is to seek to be exalted, and not the character of Christ, which is to walk in the spirit of humility. It is to show who is first among many. And since first represent the living, and last represent the dead, it is to see who is alive among the living and not last, like those who are dead and have entered their last day. The program titled, "The Last One Standing," sums it all up. When all others fall, and become like the dead, the last one standing will be the only one alive.

Satan rules in the affairs of the children of men and we are oblivious to what he is doing to us. Because he is so cunning and very subtle in his ways, he hides the real intent of his deeds in the glamor of life.

Coming under the power and dominion of the evil one, the children of this world have no clue to understand the things the ruler of this world has mounted up in the world, in which many seek their glory and take pride in their achievements. But all these things go to manifest one thing, which is *pride in exaltation*, and which was the very thing which caused the fall of Lucifer, who is now Satan, the enemy of God and man. To seek to be first and to be exalted in anything, is the way to death. But to seek to be the last and to be humble like Jesus, is the way to life eternal.

In all kinds of competition, the goal is to see who will be first, which manifests the spirit of Satan, the one who wants to be first all the time. And those who want to be first have the mark of the beast. As men are pitted one against another, and everyone seeks to win against the other, the spirit of covetousness is aroused in them. The desire to possess those prizes at stake so they can live and enjoy their bounty shows that they have not become like the dead whose possessions are given to others. As every contestant seeks to possess the prizes and goods at stake, by principle they are murderers. They are murderers because, as every one of them would rather they become the possessor of the goods at stake whilst the others have nothing, in the real sense they would rather the others were dead, since it is the dead who have nothing. Such is the character of Satan who has coveted the throne of God. And in seeking to wrestle the sovereignty of the universe from God, Satan had the Creator killed when he came to the earth as a man. In seeking to be superior to his Maker, Satan would rather be first and God last; he would rather be alive and God dead.

But the day is coming when Satan will become the last, when he shall finally come to the place of last and there die. Also, all those who have made being first their ambition and those who as fans have supported others to be first, will come to the place of last, and there, God will make them to become the last and die.

Satan has taught men to be ambitious and seek to be first, but in that day of the Lord, in the last day, God will teach every intelligent being his way to life, which is to be the last, and it will all happen in the dwelling place of God, the place of last, the last day of the week, the seventh day. In that day, "the first shall be the last and the last first."

Those who have desired to be first will become the last and those who would have lived by the principle of being last will become the first. In that last day, all the works of the wicked will come to an end and they shall die and enter rest.

The dead do not love display. They do not make a show of themselves, and they are not anxious to gain the admiration of men. In fact, being dead, they are hidden in the deep of the earth, hidden from the sight of the living.

Because of self, the lives of men are filled with pride, and we want to be seen among the living by our adornment and our status in society. The display of jewelry in the adornment of men, is not of God but the spirit of pride. God did not make our ears, noses or any part of our bodies for the display of jewelry which only goes to show the pride of life. The boring of holes in the ears, noses and other parts of the body is of the world and not of God. Moreover, the use of jewelry is not needful in adornment.

Many who claim to be believers in God, live their lives influenced by worldly trends rather than the clear word of God. They forget that their body is the temple of the Holy Spirit. And they do not realize that the Holy Spirit will not dwell in anybody who will not represent God in character and in adornment. But if we would humble ourselves like the dead who are hid from sight, our adorning will not be in jewelry and flashy clothes and unnatural colorful cosmetics. For all these things which only go to show self and the pride of life, God will come and cast to the ground the proud of the earth. Thus, the prophet Isaiah prophesied about the haughty daughters of Zion, which also refers to all the proud of the earth, saying:

> Moreover the Lord saith, because the daughters of Zion are haughty, and walk with stretched forth necks and wanton eyes, walking and mincing as they go, and making a tinkling with their feet: Therefore the Lord will smite with a scab the crown of the head of the daughters of Zion, and the Lord will discover their secret parts. In that day the Lord will take away the

bravery of their tinkling ornaments about their feet, and their cauls, and their round tires like the moon, the chains, and the bracelets, and the mufflers, the bonnets, and the ornaments of the legs, and the head-bands, and the tablets, and the earrings, the rings,and nose jewels, the changeable suits of apparel, and the mantles, and the wimples, and the crisping pins, the glasses, and the fine linen, and the hoods, and the veils. And it shall come to pass, that instead of sweet smell there shall be stink; and instead of a girdle a rent; and instead of well-set hair baldness; and instead of a stomacher a girding of sackcloth; and burning instead of beauty. (Isa. 3:16-24 KJV)

When God told Jacob to go up to Bethel and dwell there and make an altar unto God, Jacob sought to cleanse his household of the strange gods that were in their midst. He also took from his household their earrings and buried them. The scripture says:

Then God said to Jacob, Arise, go up to Bethel and dwell there; and make an altar there to God, who appeared to you when you fled from the face of Esau your brother. And Jacob said to his household and to all who were with him, put away the foreign gods that are among you, and purify yourselves, and change your garments. Then let us arise and go up to Bethel; and I will make an altar there to God, who answered me in the day of my distress and has been with me in the way which I have gone. So they gave Jacob all the foreign gods which were in their hands, and *all their earrings* which were in their ears; and Jacob hid them under the terebinth tree which was by Shechem. And they journeyed, and the terror of God was upon the cities that were all around them, and they did not pursue the sons of Jacob. (Gen. 35:1-5 NKJV)

Like Jacob and his household who traveled to Bethel to meet with God and to worship, the children of God are in a pilgrimage to that place which God has prepared for the faithful. There is the need, therefore, for God's children to put away the strange gods that are in their midst.

God has made our bodies to be his temple and dwelling place. As our bodies are to be his dwelling place, God tells us that we should not make any marks in our bodies. But because of selfish desires and ignorance of the word of God, many have defaced the temple of God with markings of tattoos and tribal marks. The counsel of the Lord says: "Ye shall not make *any cuttings in your flesh* for the dead, *nor print any marks upon you*: I am the Lord." (Lev. 19:28 KJV)

The death of Jesus was not only to save us from our sins but also to show us the way to live. When Jesus hung on the cross and cried "It is finished," it was to signify the completion of the salvation of men by his death. It was also to set an example for his followers, so they may walk as he walked, that Jesus cried out, "It is finished." When we live our lives as those who are dead, we separate ourselves from Satan and sin, and all is finished between us and our enemy. That we may be like Jesus in all things, so the apostle Paul says:

> Let this mind be in you which was also in Christ Jesus, who, being in the form of God, did not consider it robbery to be equal with God, but made Himself of no reputation, taking the form of a bond servant, and coming in the likeness of men. *And being found in appearance as a man, He humbled Himself and became obedient to the point of death, even the death of the cross.* (Phil. 2:5-8 NKJV)

It is the attempt of the enemy to use our human relationships to destroy one another by making us hurt one another by our actions and words. But if we should be as the dead, nothing can make us have feelings of resentment or bitterness towards one another.

The dead cannot hear. If we should condition our minds as the dead, there will not be an angry word that will irritate us and arouse us to anger. For the dead do not know pain or injury, neither can they be wounded by words. Even those who at the slightest irritation, will injure or kill cannot be irritated in death. Death stops their ears from hearing annoying words. You may go to them and say all kinds of annoying words to them, and they will not answer you in one. If you should ask them why they do not pick up their weapons and kill when annoying words are said to them, they will by their stillness and quietness tell you that over where they are nobody does that. They will again, by their stillness and quietness tell you, this is the place where they have come to learn all they should have learned while they were alive. And since they arrived at the place of the dead, they have learned to remain quiet when annoying words are said to them.

There is no hatred in the grave where men are humbled. In the grave, men of all races make their beds together in peace. There, their hatred for one another perishes. If we have been fools, let us go to the dead and get wisdom from them. For in the grave, even men of war lay down their weapons and embrace one another lying side by side.

The dead cannot speak. Thus, they do not speak evil of any man. For being dead, they cannot see the evil deeds of any man, and to speak about them. If we should be as the dead, we will not speak evil of any man, and it is the way of love not to reveal the evil deeds of any man. The wise man, Solomon, says: "He who covers a transgression seeks love, but he who repeats a matter separates the best of friends" (Prov. 17:9 NKJV). James, in his epistle, also says: "Do not speak evil of one another, brethren. He who speaks evil of a brother and judges his brother, speaks evil of the law and judges the law. But if you judge the law, you are not a doer of the law but a judge. There is one lawgiver, who is able to save and to destroy. Who are you to judge another?" (James 4:11-12 NKJV).

The dead do not murmur or complain, for being dead they do not know of any wrongdoing. If we should be as the dead, regardless of whatever situation in which we should find ourselves, we will not murmur. The apostle Paul, counsels, saying: "Do all things without murmuring and disputing, that you may become blameless and harmless, children of God without fault in the midst of a crooked and perverse generation, among whom you shine as lights in the world" (Phil. 2:14-15 NKJV)

The dead do not fret themselves in any way. If we should be as the dead, we will not fret ourselves when we lose time. For the dead do not know the fleeting of time, and a thousand years that has passed is but a day to the dead when they shall awake from their sleep.

You may be in line waiting to be served, and the person ahead of you being served may be taking too long to be served. Do not make faces at the person or murmur or complain. But if you should have your mental disposition as the dead, you will not be aroused to anger, neither will you think of spending too much time in line; for nothing can arouse the dead to anger. Just remember death is the way to love, and by dying, you lay down your life and all that you possess, including your time for your neighbor.

The dead are never late for any appointment with the living and they are always ready to go where the living will take them. If any are late, it is the living who are late to take the dead to the church for a burial service or to the cemetery for burial. It is said of Jesus, he never had to say, "I am sorry" to anybody. He was never late to any meeting. If we should be as the dead, who are ready for everything, we will make ample time for all our engagements and not be late.

The dead do not feel. Much as we love our loved ones and will hate to see them depart from us, if we should be as the dead, even the loss of our loved ones will not be so painful. Why? Because the dead cannot suffer from any pain or loss. It is the work of the enemy to hurt us and make us sad when we lose our loved ones. When Satan led Herodias to let Herod kill John the Baptist, it was his attempt to make Jesus sad and worried over the death of John. But when Jesus heard of John's death, the Scripture says, "he departed from there by boat to a deserted place by himself" (Matt. 14:13 NKJV). Jesus, the only man who walked perfectly here on earth, could not be disturbed by the death of John, because he lived as the dead himself and walked in perfect peace, as the dead, who have entered into rest and peace.

Our hope and prayers for our loved ones should be that whilst they are alive they live lives consecrated to God. So, even if they should depart from this life there will always be the assurance of seeing them again in the resurrection. Therefore, the apostle Paul says:

But I do not want you to be ignorant concerning those who have fallen asleep, lest you sorrow as others who have no hope. For if we believe that Jesus died and rose again, even so God will bring with Him those who sleep in Jesus. For this we say to you by the word of the Lord, that we who are alive and remain until the coming of the Lord will by no means precede those who are asleep. For the Lord himself will descend from heaven with a shout, with the voice of an archangel, and with the trumpet of God. And the dead in Christ will rise first. Then we who are alive and remain shall be caught up together with them in the clouds to meet the Lord in the air. And thus we shall always be with the Lord. Therefore comfort one another with these words. (1 Thess. 4:13-18 NKJV)

The dead do not grieve over the loss of their possessions. Because being dead, they have no more a portion in the things of the earth, and their possessions are given to the living. If we would be as the dead, we will not sorrow over our loss.

In everything, when what is rightfully yours is challenged for by another, give it up. Just remember the dead do not strive for anything, "neither have they any more a portion for ever in any thing that is done under the sun" (Eccles. 9:6 KJV)

One place of common knowledge where people lose their temper and even curse, is on the street when driving. If you are driving, and your position on the street is challenged for by another driver, do not lose your temper or curse. With a smile on your face, just give up your place to the other driver. For as the dead, you have no portion in the things of the earth. And it is the way of love to give your possessions, including your place on the street to others by laying down your life for them.

There is nothing that can disrupt the affairs of the dead. All they do is lie still in perfect peace amid the commotions of life. The winds may blow, and the rains may fall, and the earth may quake; but nothing can move the hearts of the dead to fear. Neither can the enemies of the dead threaten them to fear. They are as the rocks, unmovable.

The dead do not worry about anything and they have entered rest. We may be destitute of the means to live, but if we should be as the dead, nothing can move us to worry or to be discontented. For the dead have need of nothing, and they are anxious for nothing. We have only to heed the counsel of the apostle, Paul, saying: "And having food and raiment let us be therewith content." (1 Tim. 6:8 KJV) The apostle Paul again, says: "Be anxious for nothing, but in everything by prayer and supplication, with thanksgiving, let your requests be made known to God; and the peace of God, which surpasses all understanding, will guard your hearts and minds through Christ Jesus" (Phil. 4:6-7 NKJV).

The dead are obedient unto the living, and they go where the living will take them. If we would be as the dead, we will obey God in all his commands and every ordinance of man, as long as they do not violate the principles of God.

The God who made us also made for us food, which will sustain us and prolong our lives on the earth. After God made man, he gave to him his diet, saying: "See, I have given you every herb that yields seed which is on the face of all the earth, and every tree whose fruit yields seed; to you it shall be for food" (Gen. 1:29 NKJV). Later, when God called the children of Israel to be his children, He added meat to the diet of man, but instructed them as to what was clean for food and what was unclean. All that is unclean for food, God calls an abomination unto us. We can read the list of clean and unclean animals in the book of Leviticus, chapter 11.

Those who have surrendered their lives to God will eat only what God has given as food. They will not eat any injurious food, neither will they eat any meat God calls unclean. But they will heed the warning of the apostle Paul and keep themselves from any defilement. The apostle Paul warns the children of God, saying: "Do you not know that you are the temple of God and that the Spirit of God dwells in you? If anyone defiles the temple of God, God will destroy him. For the temple of God is holy, which temple you are" (1 Cor. 3:16-17 NKJV)

If we should eat with the knowledge of eating in consecration, for the nourishment of the body of God the Spirit, we will eat only what God has given for food. We will not eat to the excitement of our taste buds, any of those meats God calls an abomination unto us. But, rather, we will heed the counsel of the apostle Paul, where he says: "Therefore, whether you eat or drink, or whatever you do, do all to the glory of God" (1 Cor. 10:31 NKJV).

The Prophet, Isaiah, sounds a warning to the children of God, proclaiming that God will destroy every man who defiles himself with the eating of meat, which is an abomination unto us, in the judgment day of the lord. The prophet says:

For, behold, the Lord will come with fire, and with his chariots like a whirlwind, to render his anger with fury, and his rebuke with flames of fire. For by fire and by His sword will the Lord plead with all flesh: and the slain of the Lord shall be many. They that sanctify themselves, and purify themselves in the gardens behind one tree in the midst, eating swine's flesh, and the abomination, and the mouse, shall be consumed together, saith the Lord. (Isa. 66:15-17 KJV)

Death is the answer to every human problem and need. In death the poor are freed from poverty, and the hungry are freed from hunger. The sick cease from suffering, and those burdened with sorrows are set free to sorrow no more. Most important of all, in death every man is freed from sin and the domain of the enemy.

Is your life characterized by any form of evil? Do you gamble seeking to win millions of monies you can enjoy tomorrow, and that tomorrow which is not promised to you? If you do, you have not become like the dead because you do not live a life of self-denial and you are covetous for money. You do not live like the dead who have entered into their last day, and you think you have many days to live so you compete with the living for money. You also have the mark of the beast because you seek to win and grab the money at stake and all others should have nothing. By principle, you would rather be alive like the living and all others should be as the dead. Because it is the living who need money to live but the dead have need of nothing and they have nothing. Is it any wonder, that many who win millions of money through gambling, often do not live long to enjoy their prize money?

Do you jump lines? If you do, you are a thief and a murderer. You are a thief because you steal from others their position in line. And you are a murderer because by principle you consider those who are ahead of you to be dead and nonexistent and so you take their position. You also have the mark of the beast because you would rather be first and not last.

Do you go through red lights when you drive? If you do, you are a murderer and have the mark of the beast. You are a murderer, because how many accidents have been caused and how many have been killed because somebody in a hurry went through a red light. And you have the mark of the beast, because you will not come to a stop at the red light like the dead who have come to a stop in all their works.

Do you argue and insist on your opinions to be the right opinion? If you do, you are not dead and you have the mark of the beast. For the dead have given up any right to any opinion in the things of this earth.

Do you worry about anything? If you do, you have not become like the dead and you have the mark of the beast. You have the mark of the beast because you worry and you have no peace and rest for your soul. For the dead do not worry about anything and they have entered into peace and rest.

In every aspect of our lives, where we seem to be overtaken by evil, we are to apply the principle of death to our minds, that we may live the perfect life of Jesus. To this end the apostle Peter, says:

> For to this you were called, because Christ also suffered for us, leaving us an example, that you should follow his steps: Who committed no sin, nor was guile found in his mouth, who, when he was reviled, did not revile in return; when he suffered, he did not threaten, but committed himself to him who judges righteously; who himself bore our sins in His own body on the tree, that

we, having died to sins, might live for righteousness—by whose stripes you were healed. (1 Pet. 2:21-24 NKJV)

As disclosed in this book, it is evident that it is in the mysteries of death that is to be found the secret to living the perfect life, and thus, the way to be like God. If we are to win the battle against sin, we must conform to the death of Jesus. Thus, the apostle Paul says: "That I may know him and the power of his resurrection, and the fellowship of his sufferings, being conformed to his death" (Phil. 3:10 NKJV)

The death of Jesus is to be the watchword until the day of his return, to those who love his appearing. The apostle Paul, therefore, refers to the Lord's Supper and says:

> For I received from the Lord that which I also delivered to you: that the Lord Jesus on the same night in which he was betrayed took bread; and when he had given thanks, he broke it and said, "Take, eat; this is my body which is broken for you; do this in remembrance of me." In the same manner he also took the cup after supper, saying, "This cup is the new covenant in my blood. This do, as often as you drink it, in remembrance of me." For as often as you eat this bread and drink this cup, you proclaim the Lord's death till he comes. (1 Cor. 11:23-26 NKJV)

The perfect life is to be lived out in the words of this song:

> Dying with Jesus, by death reckoned mine,
> Living with Jesus a new life divine,
> looking to Jesus till glory doth shine,
> moment by moment, O Lord I am Thine.

> (Daniel W. Whittle)

# MY TESTIMONY

Several circumstances have led me to write this book. But one that is notable among them is the spiritual insight given me by the Lord into the story of David and Goliath.

After my conversion, and as I read the story of David and Goliath, the thought came to me that the story had a deeper spiritual meaning. As I pondered on the story, in an instance, in a scene that flashed through my mind, which I perceived to be a vision from God, I saw the story in a different light. I saw the giant Goliath as somebody who symbolized Satan, and David representing a man who will come and destroy Satan. So, I asked myself the question: "But who will be the David to destroy Satan?" Later, when I would see picture drawings of David standing before Goliath and ready to cast his rock at Goliath, I will point to David and say to myself, "This is me," and I will point to Goliath and say, "This is Satan." Little did I know that the thought had been put in my mind by God.

In 1982, the Lord made me to see the person of Satan in my hometown of Kumasi, in Ghana. It was not in a dream, neither in a vision, but literally as I would see any man. I did not know it was him I had seen at the time I saw him.

It all happened when I was getting ready to come to the United Sates in 1982 to further my education. I had to travel from Kumasi the city in which I lived at the time to Accra the capital city of Ghana, to finalize the processing of my papers to enable me to come to the United States.

On this eventful day, I went to the bus station in Kumasi to purchase a ticket to board a bus to Accra. Upon purchasing the ticket and as I waited for the bus, I decided to go to the cafeteria at the bus station to get something to eat. On entering the cafeteria, I saw a scene that terrified me, and which made me to stop at the door. There were many people in the cafeteria eating and drinking and talking among themselves. But at one table quite close to the door sat four men. Three of them sat with their backs towards me and with their heads turned and looking at me. After I made eye contact with them and as I looked at them, they turned and bowed their heads and began to talk among themselves, whispering into the ears of one another. But the one who sat at the head of the table looked at me with a steady gaze and with his teeth clenched and his eyes were blood-shot.

That terrifying look at me and the others whispering to one another left me with the impression that they were plotting against me. I then said to myself, "I don't know these men anywhere, but I can tell they are my enemies. I can see if I attempt to walk past them, I will not come back with my skin." So, I decided not to go and buy the food anymore. I then turned around to go and wait for the bus and all the while wondering who those men could be.

I came to the United States in April 1982 and went to the College of Charleston in South Carolina. In 1984, when I had all but forgotten about the men I saw just before I left Ghana and as I meditated on the word of God one afternoon, the Lord spoke to me, and he said: "Do you remember the strange men you saw in Ghana?" Immediately the scene flashed through my mind again, and I said, "Yes Lord. But who were those men?" And the Lord answered and said to me, "That was Satan and some of his angels." I was startled at the revelation and I pondered over it for many days.

Ten years later and in January of 1994, as I meditated on the word of God one morning, the Lord spoke to me saying, "When I made you to see Satan, I showed you to him that you will be the one to destroy him." Then I prayed and said, "Lord, you made Lucifer and you alone know how to destroy him. So give him into my hands that I may destroy him." And before I could finish my sentence, the Lord said to me in a loud voice saying, "I have given him to you!" Immediately the

Lord made me to see in a vision Satan standing and two of his angels standing before him and with their backs toward me. The two angels turned their heads and took a quick glance at me and turned their faces again to Satan and said to him, "He's destroyed us." I looked at them and I saw Satan took a long look at me from the corners of his eyes with an angry look. A few days after this vision, the Lord began to show to me the things written in this book and how to destroy the devil.

The story of David and Goliath, although a true story that happened in time many years ago, is also a prophetic story which foretells the destruction of the real Goliath, who is Satan, the enemy of God and man. For it was the spirit of Satan indwelling Goliath who with his boastings defied the armies of Israel.

In the story, Goliath represents Satan and David represents the man who filled with the Spirit of God is to come and destroy Satan. The man who has written this book is that man. The armies of Israel represent the armies of God on Earth, which are the children of God, the armies of righteousness.

The Philistines who worshiped other gods and for that reason were the children of the evil one represent the host of Satan which are evil men and the wicked angels of the enemy who dwell here on earth with us. Also, the stone with which David smote Goliath represents the true Rock, the word of God, with which the man of God will smite Satan.

The war between God and Satan first broke out in heaven. The scripture says: "And war broke out in Heaven: Michael and his angels fought with the dragon; and the dragon and his angels fought, but they did not prevail, nor was a place found for them in Heaven any longer. So the great dragon was cast out, that serpent of old, called the Devil and Satan, who deceives the whole world; he was cast to the earth, and his angels were cast out with him." (Rev. 12:7-9 NKJV)

With Satan removed from the realm of heaven and cast down to the earth, the war is no more being waged in heaven but on earth. The war is therefore being waged directly between Satan with his host of wicked angels and the children of men. So, God speaks to the inhabitants of the earth, saying: "Therefore rejoice, O heavens, and you who dwell in them! Woe to the inhabitants of the earth and the sea! For the devil has come down to you, having great wrath, because he knows that he has a short time" (Rev. 12:12 NKJV).

Goliath stood as champion in the camp of the Philistines and with his boastings defied the armies of Israel, saying: "Am I not a Philistine, and you the servants of Saul? Choose a man for yourselves, and let him come down to me. If he is able to fight with me and kill me, then we will be your servants. But if I prevail against him and kill him, then you shall be our servants and serve us…I defy the armies of Israel this day; give me a man, that we may fight together" (1 Sam. 17:8-10 NKJV).

In like manner, Satan who is the spiritual Goliath, stands as champion of the host of evil, and for these many years since the inception of sin his voice re-echoes the words of Goliath saying: "Where is the man who can fight against me?"

Besides Christ who is the Captain of our salvation and who came down to the earth to destroy Satan, no man has stood up to the boastings of Satan to say to him, "I am able to fight against you and destroy you." The man who has written this book has stood up to him.

Compared to Satan I am just a youth and he a man of war with many years of experience; just as David was just a youth in the eyes of Goliath. But I have one desire in life and that is to destroy this uncircumcised angel. Satan may come against me as a mighty angel but in the words of David I will like to say, "But I come to him in the name of the Lord of hosts, the God of the armies of righteousness who he has defied. The Lord has delivered him into my hands that I may smite him, that all the earth may know that the Lord does not deliver by sword or spear, but by His Spirit and His word which is spirit. For the battle is the Lord's, and with the knowledge He gives me do I fight."

Wars are waged with the mind and the weapons used in warfare are to manifest how we have determined to fight with our minds. Satan wages his war against us with his mind, and so we are to counter him with our minds armed with the word of God, which is the sword of the Spirit.

David was very skillful with his sling and stone, and the Lord has made me to be very skillful with his Word which is the true Rock, and with this skill do I destroy Satan. Like David who came face to face with Goliath and locked eyes with him, the Lord has made me to come face to face with Satan, to lock eyes with him, and to destroy him.

Like David who slew Goliath and cut off his head with Goliath's own sword, I have been made to destroy Satan with his own sword. The sword of Satan is death through the power of sin, as the scripture says, "the sting of death is sin" (1 Cor. 15:56). And it is with his own sword do I destroy him, who is the originator and instigator of sin and has the power of death.

Goliath had boasted and said to Israel: "Choose a man for yourselves and let him come down to me. If he can fight with me and kill me, then we will be your servants. But if I prevail against him and kill him, then you shall be our servants and serve us." (1 Sam. 17:8-9 NKJV) Like David who prevailed against Goliath to the joy of the children of Israel, God has given Satan into my hands that I may prevail against him and destroy him with his own sword to the joy of all God's children.

In December 1996, one morning as I went to one of my places of retreat for prayer and meditation, the Lord gave me a vision. In the vision, I saw a thick grey cloud hanging in the air. As I looked at the cloud, the Lord spoke to me and said, "Get a hold on the cloud." So, I got a hold on the cloud. Then the Lord said to me, "Pull it down and let go of it." So, I pulled it down and I let go of it. As I looked, the cloud began to descend dangling and swaying in an upward and downward seesaw motion. As it came closer to the ground, I looked and saw a deep pit before me, and the cloud descended and crashed into the pit with a deafening noise. I then asked the Lord, "What was that?" The Lord answered and said to me, "That is what I will let you do to Satan and his works in the things he has mounted up in the world. A few days later, the Lord revealed to me that, competitive sports and all forms of competition and the game shows, are all the works of Satan.

In the pages of this book is to be found how to destroy Satan. And it is by this way that Jesus defeated him in his life here on earth and at the cross. It is also by this same principle that God will finally destroy Satan and all the wicked. So the scripture says: "Insomuch then as the children have partaken of flesh and blood, he himself likewise shared in the same, that through death he might destroy him who had the power of death, that is, the devil" (Heb. 2:14 NKJV). Therefore, everyone who seeks to prevail against Satan and sin must be armed with death.

Satan had desired to be like the most High God, and in his temptation he had said to Eve, "You will not surely die and you will be like God." But the truth is, we can only become like God when we choose to live as those who are dead and in dying have died to sin.

Since the time the Lord began to reveal to me the secret to living the perfect life, I have suffered many things. In my sufferings, and in seeking to find an answer to all the sufferings I have been made to bear, I prayed fervently to the Lord and asked him why I was having to suffer so much. It was then that the Lord revealed to me why he allows suffering to come upon his children. I have included the things revealed to me under the chapter, "Why Suffering."

We are to become perfect only through much suffering. Satan contends that we can only keep the commandments of God or act as perfect beings only in good times, but no man can keep the commandments of God or be perfect in troublous times or in much suffering. This was Satan's contention before God when God presented Job before Satan as a perfect man and for that reason everybody who seeks to be perfect. Therefore, God allows suffering to come upon his children. It is to let his character to be vindicated in our lives as we go through sufferings.

It is through the principles of death that our characters are refined into the image of God. In every trial and suffering that God allows to come our way, God seeks to transform our characters to be like his own; unchangeable and unshakable under any circumstances, that we may be like the dead whose state of mind remains the same under all circumstances, and also like the inanimate rocks which do not know any change.

The contention of Satan about the perfect character of Job was an attack on the character of God himself. That is why God came to the earth as a man to be tempted in all ways in which the tempter tempts men. Thus it is said about the Captain of our salvation who is the True Rock: "But we see Jesus, who was made a little lower than the angels, for the suffering of death crowned with glory and honor, that he, by the grace of God, might taste death for everyone. For it was fitting for him, for whom are all things and by whom are all things, in bringing many sons to glory to make the Captain of their salvation perfect through sufferings" (Heb. 2:9-10 NKJV).

To everyone, therefore, who seeks to be like the Sinless One, comes these encouraging words by the apostle Paul, saying: "That I may know him and the power of his resurrection, and the fellowship of his sufferings, being conformed to his death, if, by any means, I may attain to the resurrection from the dead" (Philippians 3:10-11 NKJV). The apostle Peter follows the encouraging words of Paul with these comforting words: "Beloved, do not think it strange concerning the fiery trial which is to try you, as though some strange thing happened to you; but rejoice to the extent that you partake of Christ's sufferings, that when his glory is revealed, you may also be glad with exceeding joy." (1 Pet. 4:12-13 NKJV)

In the end, it will be said of those who would have endured much sufferings and yet remained faithful to God: "Here is the patience of the saints; here are those who keep the commandments of God and the faith of Jesus" (Rev. 14:12 NKJV). Here is the patience of the Saints because they have remained patient under all trying circumstances and they have not swayed away from keeping the commandments of God.

As the Lord begun to reveal to me the principles to living the perfect life, it was not till I experienced them in my life through trials and testing that I came to understand fully what the scripture means when the apostle Paul counsels us to have the mind of Christ, saying: "Let this mind be in you which was also in Christ Jesus, who being in the form of God, did not consider it robbery to be equal with God, but made Himself of no reputation, taking the form of a bondservant, and coming in the likeness of men. And being found in appearance as a man, He humbled Himself and became obedient to the point of death, even the death of the cross." (Philippians 2:5-8 NKJV).

In my experience with the principles of the perfect life, I have been made to suffer many things. I have suffered the loss of property and the mysterious deaths of loved ones. I have suffered humiliation and I have suffered being destitute.

In the beginning of the year 1994, something happened in my life. And it was through this incident that the Lord used to begin in revealing to me the principles of the perfect life.

In February 1994, a friend of mine had left his car in my possession when he traveled to Ghana, our native country. Just two days before he was due back to the United States, the car was stolen. Earlier, on the morning the car was stolen, my friend's wife called me on the telephone and asked me about the car. I gave her the assurance that the car was parked in a safe place. After talking with her, I went to get the car only to my surprise the car was not there. I made phone calls to the Police Department and the Parking Violations Department to find out if either one of these departments had the car in their possession. After finding out the car was not in the possession of either department, I realized it had been stolen. I went home and prayed and pleaded with the Lord to let me find the stolen car. I prayed and said, "Lord, nothing can escape your eyes. Even as I speak right now, you see the car and the person who stole it, and you know exactly where they are at this very moment. Please do not let this person find rest till he returns the car to the same place where he took it—or let him fall into the hands of the police, that he may be arrested."

It was hard for me to break the news of the stolen car to my friend's wife. So that day I kept going back and forth to the place where I parked the car, with the hope I would have an answer to my prayer. Nighttime came and I had still not found the car. I was then resolved to tell my friend's wife of what had happened.

After coming to the realization I was not going to find the car that day, I prayed again and said, "Lord in your wisdom, you know why you have not given an answer to my prayer in the nature of my request. Because I know nothing is impossible to you, and you could have done just as I requested of you. Therefore, let your will be done." I then went ahead and called my friend's wife on the telephone and told her of what had happened. I also gave her the assurance I was going to replace the car, since the insurance they had on the car was liability insurance. Though she was upset, she took comfort in my assurance to replace the car.

The next morning, after I had prayed again and pleaded with the Lord to let me find the stolen car, I was in deep meditation, when I heard the Lord speak to me through my mind. I heard the Lord say, "The loss of the car will be to my glory." I asked, "Lord, how will this be to your glory?" The answer came from the Lord, saying, "The dead do not suffer from the loss of their goods; for, being dead, they cannot be inflicted with pain. If you will be as the dead, you will not grieve over the loss of the car." I leapt for joy after receiving this message from the Lord. I then thanked the Lord for his marvelous answer to my prayer.

Two days after the car was stolen, my friend came back to the United States. Though he felt as his wife, he readily accepted my assurance to replace the car. A week after the car was stolen, the police called informing us they had found the car. We went and picked up the car the day after the police called.

In the meantime, after the Lord revealed to me the way to overcome pain and affliction, I pondered over it thinking about Job and wondering if he knew this secret when Satan made him to lose all his wealth and children. As I pondered over it, the Lord revealed to me how Job became an overcomer. Even though Job may not have known everything, in his trials and sufferings, he said certain things which alluded to his living by the principles of death and which are the principles of the perfect life.

In the first trial, when Satan caused Job to lose his wealth, his servants and his children, Job worshiped God and said, "Naked I came from my mother's womb, and naked shall I return there. The Lord gave, and the Lord has taken away; blessed be the name of the Lord" (Job 1:21

NKJV). It is at birth and as we live that God gives to us life and all material things. But at death everything is taken away from us; our lives and all that we possess. When everything was taken away from Job, and he was made as one who was dead, he still blessed the name of the Lord. That is living by the principle of death.

In the next trial, when Satan inflicted the body of Job with pain, Job responded by saying, "Though He slay me, yet will I trust Him" (Job 13:15 NKJV). Job had firmly decided to trust God even to the point of death. Like the dead, who are sealed in their mindset, job's mind was always sealed in trusting God. His mindset was unshakable and unmovable. He had steadied his mind to trust God till death.

Finally, in the midst of much suffering, in his closing statement, Job said, "For I know that my Redeemer liveth, and that he shall stand at the latter day upon the earth: and though after my skin worms destroy this body, yet in my flesh shall I see God: Whom I shall see for myself, and mine eyes shall behold, and not another; though my reins be consumed within me" (Job 19:25-27 NKJV). Here, Job speaks about his Redeemer, the one who redeems us from sin and death and also from all our troubles. He next speaks about worms destroying his body, which happens at death, during decay. Finally, he speaks about seeing God in this same flesh which has been destroyed by worms. Here, Job was speaking about the resurrection of the dead. By implying death and the resurrection, Job also implied the principle of baptism, which is death to sin and arising to live in newness of life, in righteousness. So, by the principles of death, Job became an overcomer.

After school and when I came up to New York to work, I bought a car to be used as a car service. I had the car in the care of a friend who was driving it for me. In about the end of March 1994, a month after my friend's car was stolen, my cab-service car was stolen. I had come back from work one evening and got the news from my friend with whom I had left the care of the cab, that the car is stolen.

After receiving the news that my cab has been stolen, I went to one of the places of my quiet retreat, which is this park near where I was living at the time. It was one of my favorite places for quiet times with the Lord and for meditation. After praying and pouring my heart to

God, I set off to go home. As I was deeply in thought, I took the time to look at the surrounding areas of the park. As I looked, I saw that at the very end of the park was a cemetery. I have been going to the park, but I had never seen the cemetery until this day. It had a high wall, which made it unnoticeable. I knew the Lord made me to see it on this day, and he had a message in it for me. I went closer to the wall and looked over the wall and saw the tombstones. Right then it was as if I were speaking to myself, but I know it was the Lord speaking to me, saying: "If the people buried here owned lands and houses and cars, they have died and left them all behind, and others have taken what is theirs. For being dead, they have no more a portion in the things of the earth." So, I said to myself, "If I should be as the dead, I do not have a portion in the things of the earth. What is mine has been taken by another and the dead do not have any knowledge of their things being taken by others. So where is the place for worry?" I filed a police report but never found the car.

In the same year, on the nineteenth day of October 1994, one of my sisters, by name Dora, who lived in Toronto, Canada, and had been very sick since the beginning of the year, died. It was hard for me to take. But I said to myself, "Ah, another loss. This time not property but life. But if I am as the dead myself, then I cannot suffer from any loss, and the dead cannot be inflicted with pain. My siblings who lived in Canada and myself living in New York, took our sister's body home to Ghana for burial.

On April 23, 1996, my mother who had been sick, also died. I had experienced practicing how to overcome the pain of loss when my sister died, and, I realized the Lord had prepared my mother for death, so I was comforted.

Another kind of suffering I was made to experience is humiliation. I came to the United States in 1982 to pursue a career in Accounting and Business Administration. It was my desire to become a Certified Public Accountant. After having furthered my education at the College of Charleston, in Charleston, South Carolina, I came to New York in 1987 in search of a job. By the grace of God, I obtained a job as an Assistant Accountant with an investment company in the financial district in New York.

When I came to New York, two of my friends, also from Ghana, who went to the College of Charleston with me, were working with the New York City Department of Transportation as Assistant Accountants. After a while, my two friends quit their jobs, leased a yellow cab and began driving the taxi, taking turns in working every other day. When I asked them why they quit their jobs, they explained they wanted to have some flexible time to enable them to study and get themselves ready for graduate school. As I listened to my two friends, I said to myself, "I will never drive a cab. What would that mean? To get some education and only to drive a cab?"

One morning as I meditated on the word of God and as I was deeply in thought, the Lord spoke to me through my mind. The Lord said to me, "Kofi, from what you have said, I can never save you into my kingdom unless you drive a cab. What do you think? Do you think you are better than those who drive cabs?" I was made to see that from what I said, I had exalted myself above everyone who drives a cab, and until I become like one of them, I am filled with pride.

After working with the investment company for a little over a year, I went to my friends and obtained information from them on how to get the license to operate a yellow cab. I got the taxi license and began to drive a yellow cab in New York City. It was here while driving a cab that I experienced many of the principles of the perfect life written in this book.

As I left my career in accounting to drive a cab, it was humiliating and humbling. But as I obeyed the rebuke of the Lord, it became a blessing and a joy. I came to realize the Lord took me where there seemed to be no dignity and there to have me behold his glory. It was here that I came to understand, how the Lord of glory, the Sovereign of the universe, came to the earth, leaving his throne above and the adoration of myriads of angels, and lived humbly as a servant. It was to reveal the principles of his character to all intelligent beings that he took on the nature of man and the form of a servant. It was here whilst driving a cab that the saying of the Lord, "I came not to be served but to serve," became practical in my own life. I saw that the Lord had taken me to a place for me to experience and understand the principles of his character.

Let me here mention a few things I learned while I drove a cab. There are more than twelve thousand yellow cabs in New York City. That means a lot of competition on the road for fares. It was here that I saw the selfish heart of man constantly at work. Sometimes some of the cabdrivers will cut in front of you from another lane to pick up a fare which was obviously your fare. At other times too, some of the drivers will race from behind you to get in front of you so they can pick up the fare ahead of you. It was here that the Lord taught me to have the mental attitude of the dead. And at such times when others would cut in front of me, I was to say to myself, "The dead have no portion in the things of the earth, and being dead they have become the last in everything." I learned to apply the principle of the last day, which is to be the last.

I have always learned to remain quiet under all adverse conditions through the various experiences I had as I drove a cab. It was here that I was made to behold the beauty in the character of God, as I was made to experience it in my own life.

With the very heavy traffic in New York City, you are usually caught in traffic with virtually nowhere to go. And sometimes you are caught behind double-parked vehicles and cabs and buses discharging or picking up passengers. Where I could have reacted impatiently by pulling my car in haste from behind stopped vehicles which could cause accidents, or to blow my horn out of frustration and anger, I learned to be as quiet as the dead, who are in no haste to go anywhere. Many times, people who rode my cab asked me why I was so calm when all other drivers around me were blowing their horns and some hurling curses.

At one time as I was driving, I came to a street with very little traffic, which I could travel on across town, but I decided to go further and go across town on a street closer to my destination, only to find it jammed with traffic. I did not repine or fret saying to myself, "Why didn't I go on the street with less traffic?" But I sat quietly in the traffic till I was able to get out of it. As I sat in the traffic, scenes of the dead flashed through my mind, and I pictured myself as a dead man in a hearse being taken for burial and caught in traffic. The dead do not fret, saying, "Why didn't we go on the street with less traffic?" But they lie still in their caskets till they reach their destination.

As I drove a cab, sometimes I will catch every red light on my trips. But during those times, I applied the principle of the dead. I will imagine myself as dead and being transported in a hearse and having to stop several times behind red lights. The dead do not fret themselves for being caught several times behind red lights but having died they are at peace and nothing can take their peace away. The dead cannot be irritated under any circumstances and they are unfazed under all situations.

As you are on the roads for long periods of time in any given day when you drive a cab, many times other drivers will cross your path abruptly from the lanes next to you. But in those times as the Lord had revealed to me the principles of his character, I began to apply them. So, in those times when others will cut me off, I applied the principles of death and last. I applied the principle of death because the dead having died have lost their sight and they cannot see anything, and neither can they be offended to be irritated by anything. Also having died, the dead have given up their portion of anything they owned in the earth including their position on the street. I also applied the principle of last because when another driver cuts you off, they come in front of you and take the first position and you come behind them and take the last position. And that is where you want to be, for the dead having died have entered the place of last and they are resting in peace, nothing bothering them. By taking the last place, you lay down your life and your possessions for your neighbor, which in this instance is your position on the street. This is also the principle of love.

The very place where I learned most of the things written in this book is the same place where I suffered the most. I have been made to suffer many things as I drove a cab. I saw that I have been placed into the furnace of affliction, to be afflicted and to be tried; to see if I would always remain as the dead, under all trying circumstances. The things I have suffered have been Satan's way of fighting against me to discourage me from realizing the fulfillment of the principles of the character of God in my life.

The wrath of Satan against me was made manifest to me by making me to get involved in several accidents. It was revealed to me that the loss of income through the numerous accidents I had and the cost of repairs were all designed by Satan to cause me to suffer much financial losses and to make living very hard for me. It was again revealed to me how Satan who has access to the minds of men, works to bring about accidents on the roads. Through a distraction on the road where a driver is distracted to take his eyes off the road, or a poor judgment on the road are all caused by Satan and his host of wicked angels to bring about accidents.

There are also those who whilst driving, will cut you off on short notice. This is something which happens to everyone who drives. It was revealed to me that Satan who has access to the minds of men is the one who causes others to cut you off in an attempt to irritate you and to make you angry. But I learned to practice the principle of the dead and being as the dead I could not be aroused to be angry.

When I look back, I count it all joy in what I have been called upon to experience. I came to see every trial as God's way of refining my character to be patterned after his own. The character of God is defined by death to sin and alive unto righteousness, which is the principle of baptism. And everyone who seeks to be like God must choose to live by the principles of death, last and rest, which in turn are the principles of the Sabbath day.

Let me at this time pose some questions to the readers of this book. You may be a business executive, or a doctor, or a lawyer, or an accountant, or a scientist, or a high-powered government official, or whatever your occupation may be. If for example, you are called upon to give up your career and work as a sanitation worker, will you readily accept it and work in that capacity? How do you regard those who perform this seemingly humiliating duty which makes life pleasant for all of us? Do you see them as your equals, or do you regard them as inferior to you? What if we should all seek to lawyers, and doctors and business executives? Who will perform the important duty of sanitation?

It is remarkable and worthy of emulation, that in the condescension of God to become a man, he did not present himself as the Lord God

Almighty, King of kings and Lord of lords of the Universe, walking among men and should be so regarded, but he took upon himself the form of a servant. Thus, the apostle Paul counsels saying: "Let this mind be in you which was also in Christ Jesus, who, being in the form of God, did not consider it robbery to be equal with God, but made himself of no reputation, taking the form of a bondservant, and coming in the likeness of man. And being found in appearance as a man, he humbled himself and became obedient to the point of death even the death of the cross." (Philippians 2:5-8 NKJV)

The King of the Universe did not come to the earth to exalt himself, but to humble himself to the point of death. When Lucifer sought to exalt himself to be as God, God humbled himself to be a servant.

As one who seeks to emulate the character of God, do you choose to be like the dead who are hidden in the grave, removed from the sight of men, and who have no portion in the things of the earth and so have become the last in everything? Or do you seek to be known as the most important person around and so you should be offered the best or first position? Do you wait to be called to serve in whatever capacity as the dead who go where they are asked to go, or do you seek to fight your way to the top? Are you willing to go where other men will take you to serve, or do you desire to go where you would want to go in your own ambitions?

All the evil in the world in its varied forms has come as a result of the ambition of the angel Lucifer who thought that being a great angel was not good enough for him, so he should ascribe to be God. But in the end, he will be without any reputation, when he shall enter into eternal death—blotted out of existence. What price to pay for foolish pride. Such will be the end of all the proud of the earth.

Given eternity to search for the mysteries of death written in this book, no man or angel could find them except the Lord reveals them to you. And for anybody to seek to be like God without getting that knowledge from God is to act the fool. For the lack of this knowledge and yet seeking to be like God in his own merit the wisest of all the created beings of God is lost, giving the sacrifice of fools and leading many, both angels and men in his folly.

Lucifer has set his heart as God, but God speaks about his certain destruction. The principle of death to sin, which he has led the human race into disobedience through deception, when he said to Eve, "You shall not surely die," is the very thing that will destroy him in hellfire, when the controversy between good and evil shall finally come to an end.

In the end of the struggle between good and evil, heaven's choir will be assembled to sing. The songbooks of Lucifer will be brought forth. The celestial choir will then sing from the songbooks of Lucifer some of the songs Lucifer, the former maestro of heaven wrote and composed with choice words in praise of the Sovereign of the universe. They shall sing songs which Lucifer wrote, taught them, and led out in singing to the praise of the Lord God Almighty. O what a name he has acquired for himself, to be called, "the former maestro of heaven." What a miserable being!  As the celestial choir sings, Lucifer will be made to listen to reflect on the time when he led them out in praising God. The songs he wrote will testify against him and his spirit will be tormented as he hears them being sang. Lucifer will then be asked the question, "Why Lucifer, why this rebellion?" Then those angels who followed Lucifer in his folly and who have acquired for themselves the name and title, "Used to worship God in heaven Folks," will be asked the question, "Aren't you the ones who sang on the celestial choir worshiping and praising God?" As they will not be able to answer, they will be asked the question, "So why this rebellion?"

Since the time the Lord started giving me the messages for this end time, he has also given me some visions. There are two of those visions which I would like to include here. In the first vision, I was doing my devotion one morning, when in a vision, I saw the Lord standing before me and holding some excessively big and heavy books. He then held out the books to me telling me to take hold of them. I was first of the impression that they must be the book of life and the book of remembrance. But to my surprise, as I took hold of them, the Lord said to me they are the song books of Lucifer. I opened the books and saw that they were the songs that Lucifer himself wrote with choice words and composed into music, which he taught to the angels of heaven and they sang them in praise of the God and Sovereign of the universe. As I stood bewildered, the Lord immediately made me to see

Lucifer standing close by and with his head bowed to the ground. I was so baffled, so, I asked him, "Is this your work?"

A few days after this first vision, the Lord showed to me another vision. In this vision, I saw that it was the period after the millennium. The Lord had descended with all the saints in the New Jerusalem. After descending, the angelic choir was assembled, and they sang many songs from the songbooks of Lucifer. After singing, they all wept bitterly and they asked the question, "so why this rebellion, Lucifer?" After this, there was a deafening silence. Soon after, God caused the fires of hell to rain on Satan, his host of rebellious angels and all the wicked of the world. Then I looked and saw that the songbooks of Lucifer were also brought forth and cast into the lake of fire.

Lucifer will be brought into the seventh and last day to bring his work to an end and there to obey the principles of the last day. Before he is finally destroyed, this troubled angel who used to worship God on the Sabbath day will be reminded of the commandment, "Remember the Sabbath day to keep it holy". In that day he will cease from sinning and it will be said to him, "Heaven is the home of the wise not fools, and the fear of God is the beginning of wisdom."

In closing, I have my ending testimonial to make. Some time ago as I meditated on the word of God, I prayed and requested of the Lord, saying, "I want to make the greatest discovery that can ever be made. By the things written in this book, I know that the Lord has answered my prayer. As I have discovered, the science of the cross is the greatest discovery that can ever be made in the whole universe. And the joy to find the knowledge of the greatest discovery, is in the words of the hymn:

> On a hill far away stood an old rugged cross
> the emblem of suffering and shame, and I
> love that old cross where the dearest and
> best for a world of lost sinners was slain.

Oh, that old rugged cross, so despised by the
world, has a wondrous attraction for me, for
the dear Lamb of God left His glory above
to bear it to dark calvary.


To the old rugged cross, I will ever be true
its shame and reproach gladly bear; Then
He will call me some day to my home far
away, where His glory forever I'll share.


So, I'll cherish the old rugged cross,
till my trophies at last I lay down.
I will cling to the old rugged cross,
and exchange it some day for a crown.

(George Bennard)